The logo design **idea book**

Inspiration from 50 masters

First published in Great Britain by

Laurence King Student & Professional
An imprint of Quercus Editions Ltd
Carmelite House
50 Victoria Embankment
London EC4Y 0DZ

An Hachette UK company

A CIP catalogue record for this book is available
from the British Library

TPB ISBN 978-1-78627-412-0

10 9 8 7 6 5 4 3 2

Picture researcher: Peter Kent
Senior Editor: Deborah Hercun
Design: Alexandre Coco

Printed and bound in China by Great Wall

The logo design **idea book**

Inspiration from 50 masters

AEG / Braun / Milan Metro / PTT / IBM / AC/DC / Leica / The Met / V&A / The Cooper Union / eBay / GERO Health / Help Remedies / Headline Publishing / Virto / Wien Modern / Restaurant du Cercle de la Voile de Neuchâtel / Crane & Co. / Obama / Volvo / Riot / Windows / Qatar / CVS Health / 23andMe / BP / NASA / LEGO / Issey Miyake's L'Eau d'Issey / Jewish Film Festival / Campari / Le Diplomate / JackRabbit / Duquesa Suites / Dubonnet / Brooklyn Children's Museum / Art UK / Art Works / Music Together / Amazon / ASME /Edition Unik / Ichibuns / Oslo City Bike / Solidarity / FedEx / 1968 Mexico Olympics / Telemundo / Nourish / PJAIT

Steven Heller and Gail Anderson

Laurence King Publishing

Contents

Introduction: Idea + identity = logo

Logos are the most ubiquitous and essential of all graphic design devices. They are designed to include at least one, if not more, of the following components: words, letters, shapes and pictures. In addition, logos often draw from a lexicon of universal visual elements, such as arrows, swashes, swooshes, globes, sunbursts, and parallel, vertical and horizontal lines. Alternatively referred to as a mark, sign, seal or emblem, a logo is usually produced and applied to various physical manifestations, including flags, banners or shields, and appears printed, engraved or inscribed on virtually all surfaces in any configuration and on various materials in two or three dimensions.

Logos (or logotypes as they are known when type is the primary element) *represent* ideas, beliefs and, of course, things. They primarily identify products, businesses and institutions but they are also associated, hopefully in a positive way, with the ethos or philosophy of those entities. Logos are, however, vessels; they are *not* inherently good or bad, sacred or profane, but rather symbolic depictions of what they are used to characterize. They may be abstract or figurative, but logos embody a specific intention. In this sense, logos must have a purpose or a defined goal – they must exude power. The function of logos is to capture attention, foster recognition and, if successful, induce loyalty. A logo cannot be without character and must be demonstrative, active and vivid.

'A logo does not sell, it identifies', wrote Paul Rand, the designer of IBM, Westinghouse and scores of other logos. A modern logo is rarely a description of a business, as it was when trademarks used pictures to literally illustrate the nature of a business. 'A logo derives meaning from the quality of the thing it symbolizes, not the other way around', he added, arguing that a logo is 'less important than the product it signifies'. Because what it represents is more important than what it looks like, the subject matter of a logo can be almost anything.

Good design is not irrelevant to logo design, yet paradoxically a good logo is not always a well-designed one. Because the first goal of any logo is to attain memorability that is further associated with what it represents, the result is not always measured by aesthetic standards. Although acceptance of mediocrity is antithetical to the essence of design, an awkwardly composed device could just as easily become memorable and impactful as an elegantly produced one. Still, the idea behind a logo must be sound.

The 50 logos in this book are examples of good ideas in the service of representation. Aside from the inevitable debates over the choices of typefaces, colours or other graphic elements – which are subjective expressions of preference or taste – behind every strong logo there must be a solid idea that stands up to scrutiny. The ideas addressed here are the foundations on which logos are ultimately built. The rest, whether it is good or bad, memorable or forgettable, is up to the viability of the establishments they represent.

Give personality to letters

AEG / Braun / Milan Metro / PTT / IBM / AC/DC / Leica / The Met / V&A / The Cooper Union / eBay / GERO Health / Help Remedies / Headline Publishing / Virto / Wien Modern / Restaurant du Cercle de la Voile de Neuchâtel

AEG
Letters as nameplate

Letters can be read as words, initials or symbols. But when Peter Behrens became design director and artistic consultant for the Allgemeine Elektricitäts-Gesellschaft (German Electricity Company) in 1907 the honeycomb logo he designed was not just a stack of letters: it was a mark that altered the way trademarks or logos were constructed.

Behrens was an architect who understood that a corporation was a conglomeration of many design segments – graphic, poster, catalogue, advertisement, product, interior, building and type – that were best communicated to the consuming public through a sense of unity, a very specific unified discipline that equalled a whole corporate story and separated it from any competitors. This AEG identity system, which unintentionally influenced Adolf Hitler's adoption of the swastika as the symbol to unite the Nazi Party and German nation, projects the personality of the company without using its lengthy, tongue-twisting name. The AEG logo builds a brand without overstatement and lends a certain finesse to the entire entity.

Behrens was fortunate to have three letters to work with. The composition of the three letters AEG suggests a triangle that is enclosed in other geometric containers. The ease with which it is read is not just easy on the eye, it is memorable too, which for him was essential for preserving the communications integrity of a multi-faceted modern business. Behrens began with the logo and from that he created a complex corporate identity, becoming the first to combine art and industry as it is practised today.

☒ Peter Behrens, 1907

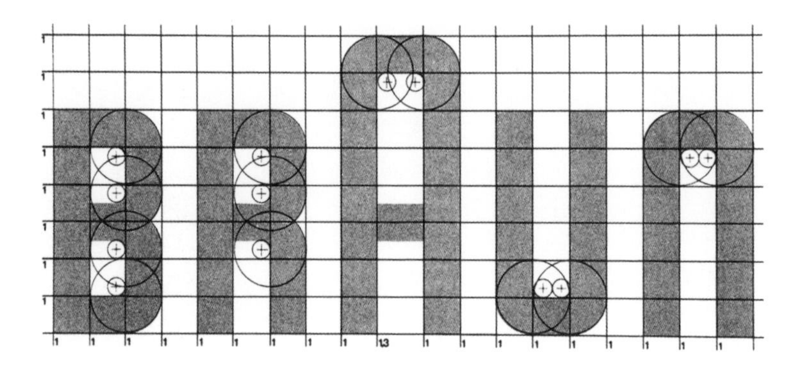

☒ Will Münch, 1934
(revised by Wolfgang
Schmittel, 1952)

Braun
The ‘A’ that looks like a radio

The eponymous German manufacturing company began in Frankfurt am Main in 1921 as a small engineering shop founded by Max Braun, a mechanical engineer. In 1923 he began producing components for radio sets and five years later, taking advantage of new discoveries in plastics, the company had moved to a factory in the same city. It was there that Braun began to manufacture entire radio sets and became one of Germany’s leading radio manufacturers.

The raised ‘A’ goes back to the design of the Art Deco-style radio housing of the ‘Cosmophon’ from 1932–3 and links the name with the radios. In 1934 the ‘Braun’ trademark was launched and the original iteration of its simple, geometric, modern wordmark – with the raised, curved middle letter ‘A’ – was designed by Will Münch.

During World War II the Braun factories were destroyed in Allied bombings. After the war, the rebuilt Braun continued to produce state-of-the-art radios and audio equipment, and soon became well known for its high-fidelity record players and straight-tray (as opposed to round-tray) models. Braun’s stellar reputation owed much to the product designer Dieter Rams, and the company capitalized on this aesthetic appeal to consumers when the S50 electric shaver was released in 1950.

The logo has remained fairly consistent throughout its history, with few refinements. In 1952 Wolfgang Schmittel revised the logo by giving it a reduced, constructively comprehensible form. In 1955 the typeface Akzidenz-Grotesk, introduced by Otl Aicher, was the only font to be used for print communication. After Rams retired in 1995 the original logo was redesigned by Peter Schneider (used from 1995 to 2005).

Today, the logo is the embodiment of the values of a corporation that has grown and changed hands. According to American logo designer Tom Geismar: ‘The Braun logo has been around for so long, and it is always associated with sleekly designed products, on which it is always discreetly placed. So in a way it represents smart modern product design.’

Milan Metro
Coordination and synchronization

Creating an identity for a city's transit system is not simple. Developing the logo is just one small piece of a larger, labyrinthine task that involves the coordination and synchronization of multiple design components. Bob Noorda was an identity designer with a particular skill for graphically modernizing subway systems. In 1954 he moved to Milan and then in 1965 he co-founded, with Massimo Vignelli, Unimark International in Chicago. By 1966 the men were redesigning the signs for the New York City Subway; according to Pagan Kennedy, writing in *The New York Times*, 'they invented what they thought of as a new grammar for New York City .... They used minimal text, arrows only when necessary and colour-coded discs to indicate different train lines. The discs were Noorda's masterstroke.'

Several years before, in 1962, Noorda's first subway commission had been for Milan's Line 1. Franco Albini, the Italian Neo-Rationalist designer-architect, asked Noorda to design not simply a logo but an entire wayfinding system for the subway he was building. He devised a striking, colour-coordinated band that stretched along the walls inside each station. A red band every five metres (16 feet) identified the station name, while a second band provided exit and transfer directions and safety signs. A sans serif font was designed for greater coordination and legibility. In 1964 Noorda was one of the winners of the Compasso d'Oro industrial design award for his work in Milan. Regrettably, the visual flag of the design – his elegant double-'M' logo, with curves inspired by Albini's fluid station railings – was scrapped due to politics within the transit agency. Noorda's overall design has since been replaced by the clumsy use of brighter colours and less-coordinated typefaces; at street level, the light boxes that indicate the station's entry stairs have had their sublime, curvilinear 'MM' substituted with a simple 'M'.

'Stupid is the word. Stupid because they have no notion of the idea behind certain choices', Noorda wrote in *Bob Noorda Design* (2015). 'I had used matte paint for the red panels, now they're using gloss that's so dazzling you almost can't read the sign. They're also using a different typeface from the original, far less interesting than the one I had designed.'

⊠ Bob Noorda, 1964

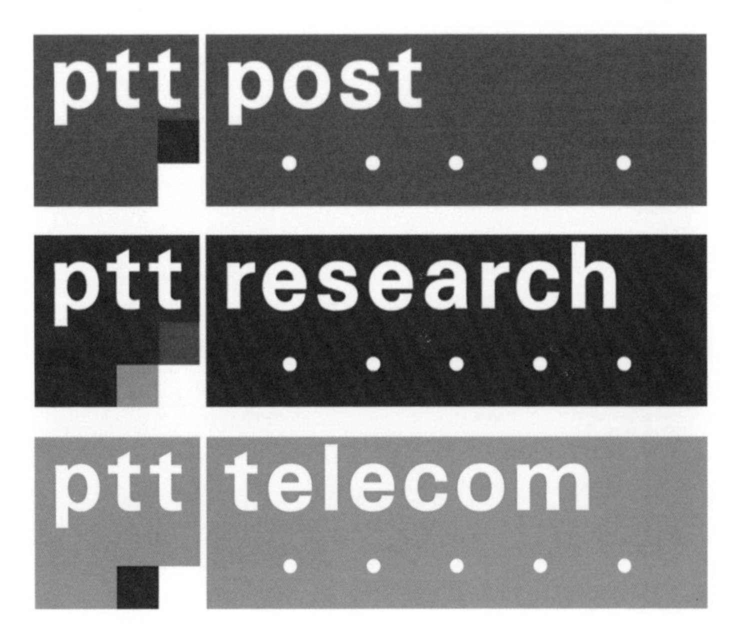

⊠ Studio Dumbar, 1989

PTT
Classic yet timeless

In terms of design, one of the most progressive nationalized services in twentieth-century Europe has been the postal and telecommunications company PTT in the Netherlands. Not only was it a wellspring of avant garde design (for example, Piet Zwart's 1938 *Het Boek van PTT* was a children's book replete with typographic experimentation), but it has also presented a consistently exciting programme of brand identity, from stamps to stationery. Since PTT was privatized in 1989 its logo has been at the forefront of its strategy.

The design was the work of Studio Dumbar in The Hague. The brief was to reinforce the relation of the divisions to each other within an overall system. It was also necessary to remain loyal to elements of the earlier house style that included Univers type in a square.

The designers developed drawings that deconstructed, rescaled and layered the core elements. The foundation of the new PTT logo is a grid of squares reminiscent of the Dutch 1920s De Stijl movement. Gert Dumbar notes that the goal was anti-clarity because clarity can be very boring, as he told *Eye* magazine: 'This brings the new clarity of uniqueness, with dogmatic forms that you can play with in a non-dogmatic way.'

The three basic logotypes are PTT Post, PTT Telecom and PTT Nederland. 'Each has the letters "p t t" in a modified Univers 65 typeface set in white with a coloured square box', explained Hugh Aldersey-Williams in *Eye*, referring to the box conceit: red for the Post, green for Telecom or blue for the five other divisions. 'Adjoining the box and separated from it by [a] white rule is another box three units long. Into this rectangle go the division titles and a row of five dots spaced according to the square grid. These are used for registration when affixing subtitles. The dots also hint at the Morse of telephony and [the] perforations of stamps.'

The Dumbar identity retains strict typographic and geometric parameters, but unlike many corporate identity standards there remains room for play in the numerous ancillary and support materials. PTT properties, including trains, cars, uniforms and coffee mugs, use differently scaled logos applied to surfaces with a certain spirited abandon.

IBM
Indelible stripes

It has been widely speculated that when Paul Rand added the emblematic lines to the IBM logo it was to symbolize computer technology. But symbolism was not a motivation in this instance; Rand himself insisted: 'The trademark becomes doubly meaningful when it is used both as an identifying device and as an illustration, each working hand in hand to enhance and dramatize the effect of the whole.' The 'scan lines' served two pragmatic ends: memorability and contrast.

IBM's mark before Rand was set in Beton Bold, a slab serif with nineteenth-century antecedents. Rand realized the folly of a radical change because the mark was already recognizable to its customers, so his initial means to improve legibility was to replace Beton in 1956 with a more modern version called City, designed by Georg Trump. Rand then customized the shape of the letterforms: he lengthened the serifs and made the stacked squares in the letter 'B' larger. The relationship between these three charged letters had to be of the highest quality.

He further ensured that when others used the logo they did not make any mistakes. In a 1969 article that appeared in *Print* magazine he wrote about precision: 'Quality deals with the judicious weighing of relationships, with balance, contrast, harmony, juxtaposition, between formal and functional elements – their transformation and enrichment.'

In 1972, after refreshing IBM with the City typeface, he introduced two versions (eight and 13 lines) of the striped logo. 'Given the problems of sameness, of anonymity of a common language of design, the need for a distinctive means of company identification is abundantly clear', he wrote in the corporate booklet *Use of the Logo/Abuse of the Logo: The IBM Logo, Its Use in Company Identification.* Rand prohibited alterations – only he was allowed to play with the logo, as he did with the famous rebus illustrated here. Otherwise the stripes, used today, continue as the logo's memorable asset.

⊠ Paul Rand, 1981 (rebus variation of his iconic 1972 logo)

AC/DC

AC/DC
Type makes the band

Besides their heavy metal music, AC/DC was defined by the logo designed by Gerard Huerta, a lettering artist from California. His first encounter with the band was in 1976, when Bob Defrin, creative director for Atlantic Records, had him render lettering for the band's first American album release called *AC/DC High Voltage*. At 25, Huerta was a neophyte freelancer and he explains this was basically his illustrative interpretation of the title: 'The AC and DC leaned toward each other with the subhead drawn in lightning-bolt style lettering on a circle, anchored to the sides of the album by rules.' The lightning bolt had appeared on their earlier Australian releases, but Huerta was now making it a more-prominent element.

☒ Gerard Huerta, 1977

Usually, an album had a theme or title and it was Huerta's job to interpret that through his letterforms. He designed lettering for the next AC/DC album entitled *Let There Be Rock*, an obvious reference to a biblical verse. This AC/DC album cover featured the band on stage with a dark sky overhead and light shining divinely down through the clouds. One of his sketches was based on ecclesiastical typography and in particular the gothic lettering famously used in Johannes Gutenberg's famous moveable type-printed Bible. He had designed lettering for Blue Öyster Cult a couple of years before based on a similar idea. That lettering took on a slightly menacing look that, Huerta says, became the beginnings of heavy metal lettering.

'I decided to render it in orange and bevel it dimensionally to complement the blue cast of the sinister sky', he says about the only hand lettering he designed that was made entirely of straight lines. The lettering was designed specifically for this album.

The logo was used on more than 20 million album covers and merchandise. Ever since, it's been used on anything to do with the band. It is a huge part of their mystical, almost religious, appeal; generations later, fans still spend US$20 for an AC/DC T-shirt because of Huerta's logo. 'I was paid what was fair for an album lettering job at the time. It was done for a specific album. They used something else for a follow-up album, then came back to this.' The original artwork is in a box in Huerta's archives, untouched.

Leica
A product of its time

No one really knows who designed the famous Leica camera wordmark. The logo seems to have anonymously materialized – a product of its time that has passed the test of time.

In 1864 Ernst Leitz, a creator of high-precision microscopes, became a partner of the Optisches Institut in Wetzlar, Germany, and in 1869 he founded his own optical company, Ernst Leitz GmbH. His son, also Ernst, became head of the company upon his father's death in 1920, and remained in charge until his own death in 1956. As early as 1911 the younger Ernst experimented with making a portable camera, and soon expanded the company's production to include cameras. The brand name Leica was created from the first three letters of Ernst's surname and the first two of the word camera: lei-ca.

Ernst is presumed to have selected the script logo as a 'signature', and years afterwards the unmistakable letters were placed inside the circle known as the 'red dot', which has become the indelible Leica symbol. In a 2011 advertisement the company claimed that the red dot and the script type have not changed since 1913. Nor has the premium quality of the product.

However, the fact is that the first logo – for what was originally called E. Leitz Wetzlar – is set white on black in a rectangle. There are then black Leitz logotypes without a circle, with the name Wetzlar (and another with Canada) in a cap sans underneath; versions in a circle only began to appear in the 1970s, and only one was red. The Leica font started out as a script with a flamboyant swash on the bottom of the 'L' in the style of the Leitz logo. These letters appeared in rectangles as well as circles. In 1996 the red dot appeared for the first time as a company logo designed by Stankowski + Duschek, who also added the name Leica in black capital letters. In 1999 the dot, with and without the name Leica, finally became the company's sole logo.

Type designer and design writer Erik Spiekermann writes that today the red Leica circle is a symbol of innovation and quality. 'The product is the brand, and the brand is the company' – a finely tuned brand built on timeless quality and innovation that keeps Leica at the forefront of image-making today.

☒ Designer unknown, 1913

THE
MET

The Met
Smash and abbreviate

It is a common trope among businesses and institutions alike to shorten or abbreviate their names. Primarily it helps to modernize a venerable organization through staccato or lyrical cadence, less official informality and other perceptual virtues. Sometimes it simply sounds and looks better in an abbreviated form.

The Metropolitan Museum of Art in New York is the epitome of the city's cultural tradition, with its imposing Beaux-Arts façade and Gothic Revival architecture that date back to its opening on Fifth Avenue in 1880. Since 1971 the museum's logo had been a Roman letter 'M' situated in the classic geometric schematic used by Renaissance draughtsmen and originally designed by Luca Pacioli, who worked with Leonardo da Vinci. The 'M' represented the classical focus of the institution, in contrast to the city's contemporary Museum of Modern Art (MoMA) and Whitney Museum of American Art, each of which have modern logos. That changed in 2016 when a new mark was unveiled to relentlessly severe criticism. *New York* magazine headlined a story: 'The Metropolitan Museum of Art's New Logo is a Typographic Bus Crash.'

Created by the branding firm Wolff Olins, this mark was not a 'refresh' but an entire brand overhaul and the introduction of a new graphic language. More inviting to the general public, the new wordmark is ostensibly two ligatures. Stacked in equal size and weight, each separate word – 'THE' 'MET' – shares common verticals and horizontals. The two words are printed in red, which *New York* magazine admonished 'looks like a red double-decker bus that has stopped short, shoving passengers into each other's backs'.

⊠ Wolff Olins, 2016

The identity scheme (which includes THE MET Breuer – the old Marcel Breuer Whitney, now showing the modern collection) does succeed by focusing attention on what visitors have long called the museum anyway: The Met. The smashed letter or ligature conceit gives the mark its mnemonic power and whereas the classic 'M' exuded an institutional mustiness the current logo expresses both continuity and change.

V&A
The missing piece

The Victoria and Albert Museum, established in 1852 as the Museum of Manufactures, has played a significant role in the heritage of British art and design. In 1990 the museum's logo was given an update by Alan Fletcher, co-founder of Pentagram London. His mandate was simple: create a recognizable mark that communicates the museum's past and present. The museum had generated too many identity marks over the years, causing confusion; so to end that the trustees had commissioned one new logo as an umbrella for the entire museum. The brief regulated that the design should comprise three characters (V&A) and be 'functional, dateless, memorable and appropriate'.

The typography he selected projects a classic with modern aesthetic by using the Bodoni typeface, which was created 200 years ago by Giambattista Bodoni in Parma, Italy. It telegraphs a sophisticated and elegant presence that is in sync with the museum's overall image.

Fletcher made some minor adjustments to the typeface, removing one of the legs on the left side of the 'A'. This conceit gives the logo its intriguing personality. By toying with the viewer's expectations, Fletcher played a perceptual game that serves as a mnemonic: at first it looks like a normal 'V' and an 'A' – then it becomes clear that something is missing, yet the eye fills in the gap.

For a logo to be effective it must serve as an unambiguous symbol of what it represents. In this case the mark captures the Victoria and Albert Museum by being classic yet not rigidly so. Fletcher has designed a brand that is not flashy but still illuminates what it symbolizes, simply because it is at once a classic type and a contemporary monogram. That the logo is a success is underscored by the fact that it is used in the many different advertisements and information booklets associated with the V&A.

☒ Alan Fletcher/Pentagram,
1990

V&A

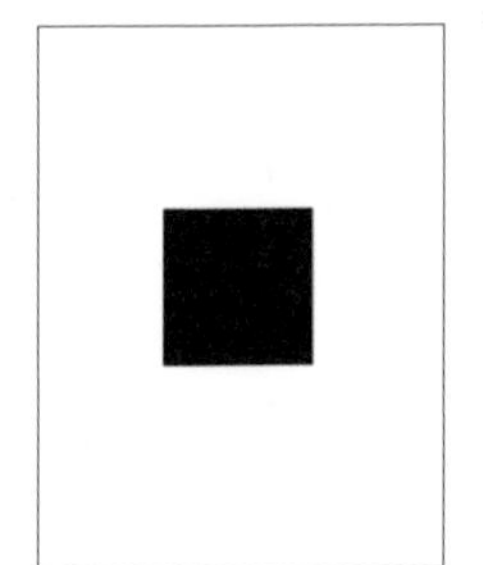
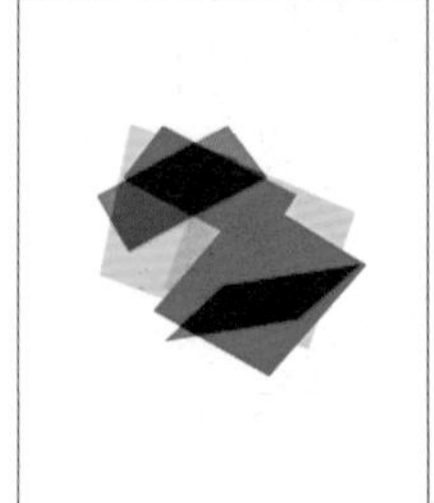

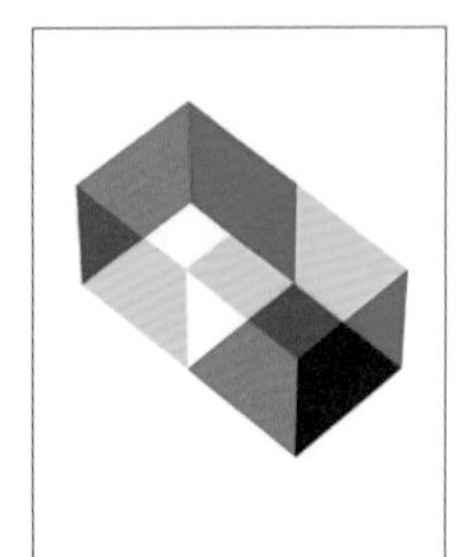

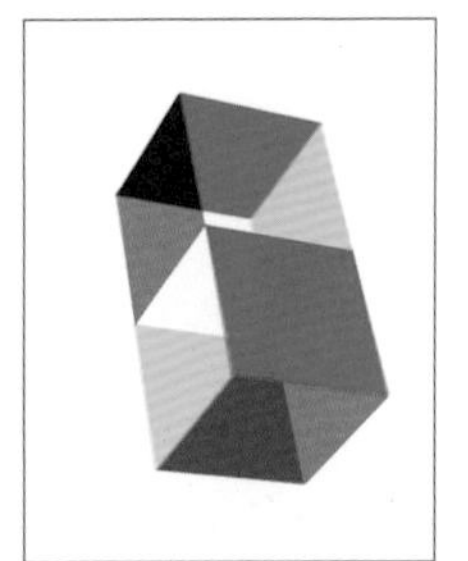
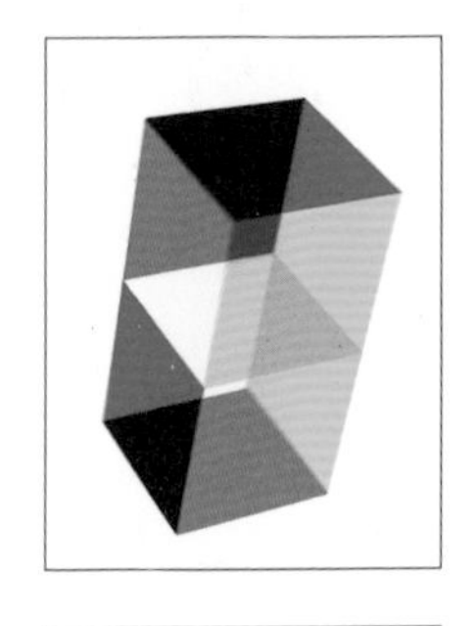

THECOOPERUNION

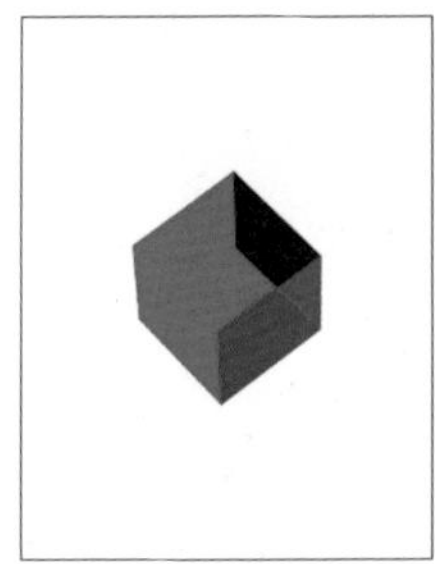
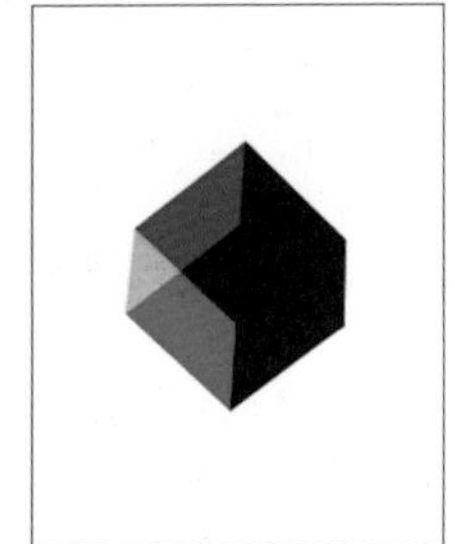
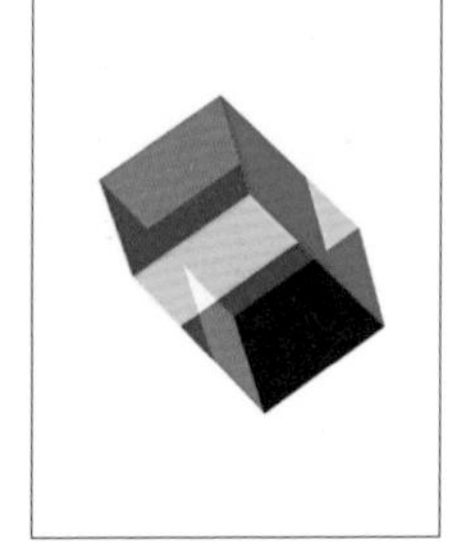
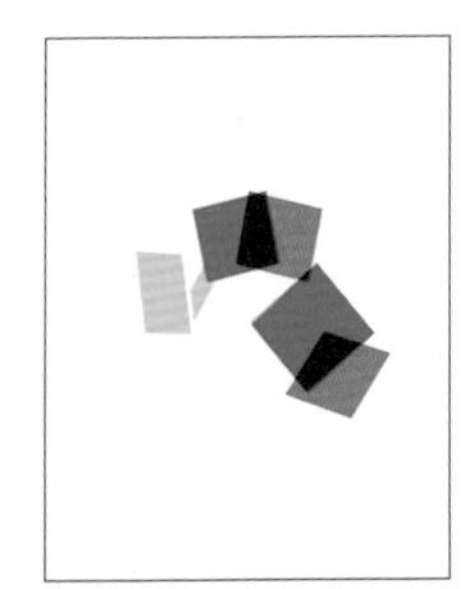
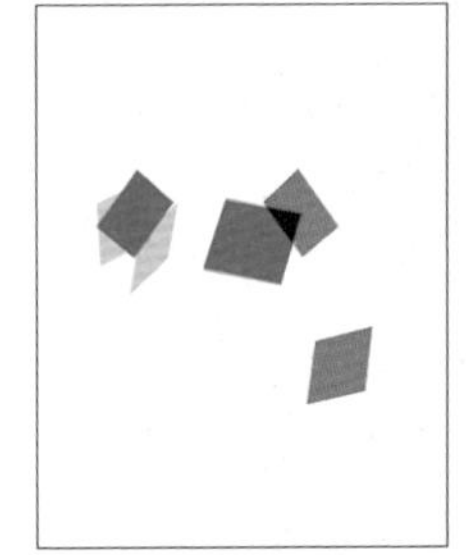
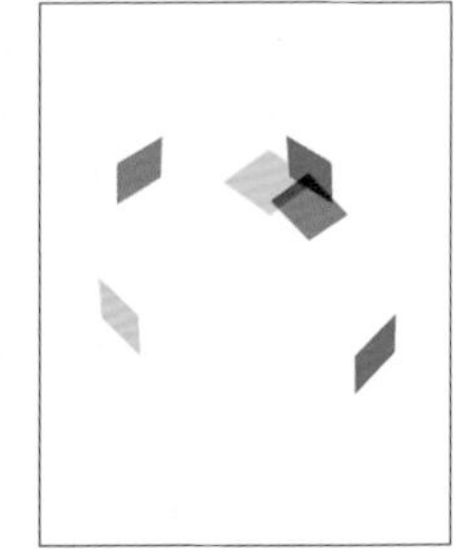
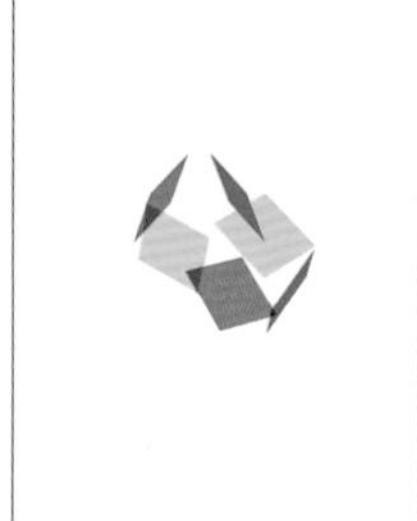

The Cooper Union
Abstractly embracing the future

With a new academic building on Cooper Square that opened in 2009, angularly designed by the Pritzker Architecture Prize winner Thom Mayne, it was decided that a fresh identity was imperative. Stephen Doyle, a graphic designer and Cooper Union alumnus, created the animated, transparent, abstract and joyful mark to express history, tradition and culture, embrace the future and echo the shapes of the new building.

Doyle also had to symbolize the schools of art, engineering and architecture. His task was to represent science and art, or 'two sides of the brain' in a single icon, and he began by exorcising the ghosts of the old traditional academic logo. Doyle used light and transparency to suggest the intersection of art and science. He tapped into his own imagination, assisted by digital software that enabled him to make a curiously fluid object out of the letters 'C' and 'U'. The result is an animated logo that begins with a typographic reference point and, using layers of primary, transparent colour, morphs into an abstract form – a three-dimensional box, with open and closed sides, that looks a lot like a box kite and floats above the words 'The Cooper Union'. The box is free of gravity, suggesting imagination and play.

Doyle's logo is irrationally rational. The colours could represent the three different schools that comprise the school, and the two shapes (the 'C' and the 'U') could be science and art. 'But,' he said, 'they are also just aesthetically pleasing.' The logo is designed to be animated on the Cooper Union's website, but even when it is not (as in print materials), its juxtaposed colours make it appear to flicker, which is simply fun to behold – assuming one is not susceptible to migraines. The fact that the 'CU' morphs into a complete abstract object can't help but trigger a smile.

Stephen Doyle, 2009

eBay
Digital stimulation

When the Internet began to change people's lives in the 1990s one of the early drivers was eBay, the online market to buy, sell and auction everything imaginable. Pierre Omidyar, the company's founder, had originally used the name Echo Bay Technology Group but when he found the domain name echobay.com had already been taken, he fortuitously shortened it and established the website name as eBay. A logo with vibrant, playful, primary 'eBay colours' and touching letters – one that eBay president Devin Norse Wenig told *Adweek* represented 'our connected and diverse eBay community' – was developed and retained for 17 years. *Adweek* magazine stated that the logo was considered 'butt ugly' but iconically recognizable.

In 2012 it was refined, albeit cautiously. A less-chaotic eBay logo using a lower-case, sans serif type was designed by the creative consultancy Lippincott. *Adweek* noted: 'Toning down the logo is likewise meant to be metaphorical – with the streamlined mark embodying a "cleaner, more contemporary and consistent experience" offered by eBay.'

Public acceptance of the new mark was immediate, and the familiarity of the basic components did not confuse its loyal users. Retaining the same colour combination and refining the conceit of slightly nudging the four letters together was a calming refresh of the original, indicating that the digital brand had not changed so much as grown from being the early digital pioneer into a solidly successful digital brand playing on the international stage.

Paul Rand had observed that logos, with their inherent mystique, are 'rabbits' feet' – and 'you don't mess around with rabbits' feet', especially in a quickly changing digital universe where consumer loyalty is mercurial. The leadership of eBay realized the need to redefine the company's tried-and-true logo in order to represent new offerings, including the new tools for buying and selling in the eBay marketplace. 'It was not a decision they entered into lightly', noted Lippincott.

ebay®

⊠ Lippincott, 2012

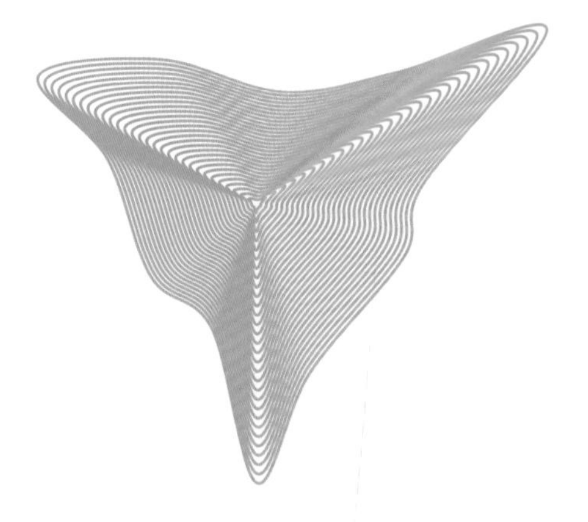
GƐRO

GƐRO

HI, WELCOME
TO GERO.
THE BEST WAY TO IMPROVE YOUR LIFE.
I HAVE A
DEVICE
I WANT TO
BUY ONE
DEMO
MODE

GERO Health
A generative tree of life

GERO is a Russian biotech healthcare startup that in 2013 developed a new digital technology adapted from mathematical models to identify age-related diseases early on, based on an analysis of the user's daily activity.

Berlin-based design consultancy think moto developed a flexible visual identity to create the focal mark: a generative logo that is created from the movement data of users to produce a changing, abstract tree of life. The shape of the figurative form recalls sigma, the letter of the Greek alphabet that is used as the sign in mathematics for sum. 'And indeed, the logo is exactly that,' says think moto's Marco Spies, 'the sum of all data from the GERO community.'

In the initial strategy phase think moto developed three core brand attributes: connecting – linking body with mind and people with people; ingenious – acting creatively smart in every situation; and precise – scientifically exact and to the point. They created the visual appearance based on this. The core image, a three-axis star, suggests the mythical symbol of the tree of life. Spies adds: 'It is a widespread archetype in the world's mythologies, symbolizing favourable living circumstances that secure a good life.' The logo itself was first developed as a physical paper prototype before being coded in processing.

The three axes of the logo are in constant movement, reflecting the activity of the GERO community and each member's personal activity generated through the app. Each axis corresponds in real time to one of three spatial axes (x, y and z). The colours are generated based on the overall health condition of the GERO community (for example, stress, condition and age).

☒ think moto, 2013

Along with the logo, think moto worked in parallel on the user experience/user interface (UX/UI) for the digital product, a mobile app for monitoring the user's personal health state. Because of the technology that was necessary for success, the entire project required a team of engineers and mathematicians who were highly committed and very passionate about their subject.

Help Remedies
Relieving headaches through simple design

In 2012 Help Remedies, Inc., a New York-based pharmaceutical startup company, launched a line of 'minimal' or single-ingredient, non-prescription medications. A sleeping pill was just a sleep aid and a pain reliever was also just a pain reliever, with no additional dyes, coatings or deleterious added medications. Each product has just one active ingredient in each pill. Co-founders Richard Fine and Nathan Frank announced: 'We felt that there was a need to make healthcare in general simpler, easier, friendlier, more human.'

To achieve this, and to create a visual distinction that sets the generic-sounding Help Remedies brand apart, a unique logo was employed. The simple lower-case 'help' is integral to its product packaging, which instead of a brand title includes easy-to-understand phrases, like 'I have a headache', 'I can't sleep', 'I have a sore throat', and more, all in the same type style. Pearlfisher, an independent global design firm, designed the ground-breaking approach and all products are packaged in a flat, white, textured hinged case with a snap-shut mechanism. The textures indicate the shape of the pills inside, alongside the different brand and symptom statements in distinctively coloured typefaces. It does not look like a conventional medications range, but as a brand family it holds together as an entirely fresh line of products.

'We are committed to using our design expertise to remove waste and reduce the environmental impact of everything we create,' said Pearlfisher Creative Director, Hamish Campbell. 'We worked with Help Remedies to refresh the packaging and introduce variant to its portfolio.' As part of the rollout, they launched the laudable Take Less campaign, and Pearlfisher's new packaging for the product range evoked a sense of safety and concern, which has not been one of Big Pharma's key selling points.

Jonathan Ford, Pearlfisher Creative Partner, added: 'Our design team refined the existing identity, colour-coding the embossed pill shape to visually strengthen the brand architecture, improving stand-out and immediacy of recognition.'

Following the redesign, sales increased 1,000 per cent, delivering on the goal to create broader desire around the Help Remedies brand.

☒ Pearlfisher, 2008

HEADLINE

MIDDLETON
FOX
OLLERTON
MACLACHLAN
SAS
WHO DARES WINS
LEADERSHIP SECRETS FROM
THE SPECIAL FORCES
NEIL GAIMAN
BLACK DOG
EAGLES
OF·THE
EMPIRE
XV
SIMON
SCARROW
INVICTUS
NEIL GAIMAN
AMERICAN GODS
GEORGE
LUCAS
A LIFE
BRIAN JAY
JONES
MARTINA COLE
BETRAYAL
MC
IT'S IN THE BLOOD

Headline Publishing
A hidden exclamation of power

It is a special gift – for both the graphic designer and the audience or recipient of a design – when good fortune enables a graphic or alphabetical element to be hidden within a logo and become a built-in mnemonic. FedEx (page 112) expresses this conceit well with its hidden arrow and has received a lot of attention in the 'logo world' for it. But the letter mark for Headline Publishing Group stamps an extra-special exclamation point onto this kind of optical illusion. At first glance the stylized Headline 'H' is just a capital letter 'H'. Yet once deciphered it becomes possible not to see the 'H' at all, but only the subtly camouflaged exclamation point emerging from the negative space. This is most obvious in their use of the logo on their paper shopping bag.

The logo was commissioned to mark the 30th anniversary of the UK book publisher, founded in 1986. A bold, arguably architectural, 'H' with a low crossbar reveals the exclamation mark as vivid as can be. The design, which appears on the spines of books and all company materials, is intended to match the publisher's self-professed 'modern and energetic nature' – and is, in fact, interpreted by some to mirror the look of the London publisher's offices at Carmelite House, the modern concrete-and-glass structure it moved to in 2015.

Patrick Insole, the art director of Headline Publishing Group, told *The Bookseller*: 'We wanted to develop a bold and colourful new brand that captures the passion, energy and pride that we all feel in working for Headline.' Working with Magpie Studio, an innovative, London-based brand consultancy, they have created what Insole describes as 'a confident and distinct new identity that is a stylish reflection both of our unique vision and our commercial sense of fun'.

☒ Magpie Studio, 2016

This is a lot to ask of a mark. Yet Headline's rebrand is designed to inspire and encapsulate the publishing company's ambitions. 'The first 30 years have been terrific, and our new look marks a fresh chapter', said Insole.

Virto
The future as typeface

In the early 1960s a TV cartoon series called *The Jetsons* projected a farcical vision of life in an automated, computer-reliant future. Today that future is more or less reality. Axiare Patrimonio, a property asset management company, developed the Virto Building, located in Alcobendas near Madrid and now owned by Inmobiliaria Colonial. Virto is the first plugged-in corporate space in Spain to employ a state-of-the-art virtual assistant throughout the offices. It is an intelligent digital system with voice-activated apps, touchscreens and movement control scanners. Users will be able to address myriad virtual services in the workplace through their smartphones. The technology was developed by Axiare's own innovation lab, Axiare R+d+i.

The branding for Virto was created by SUMMA, which started with a strategic concept that included devising the building's name (suggesting a sense of the virtual), designing its identity, including an alluring typographic wordmark, and then overseeing the ways it would be telegraphed. Rather than focus on the notion of 'an ostentatious or futurist high-tech workspace', the identity underscores instead that all the technological advances and benefits improve the quality of life of the people who use the building. And because the building must appeal to the world's most advanced companies, the Virto brand was designed to be consistent with their values and culture; a brand that transmits a cutting-edge technological aura.

The Virto logo and identity ancillaries were inspired by the shapes in the work of the Spanish painter and sculptor Pablo Palazuelo, whose twentieth-century art movement Trans-geometría sought to translate the organic rhythms of nature into plastic art. This philosophy also influenced the design of the building's façade and interiors. In an association between its corporate identity and its architecture, the designers identified in the artist the bond between graphic design and architecture. SUMMA wanted the typeface to reflect the attitude of the building. Palazuelo's changing lineal rhythms provided them with a visual language to create a fluid brand, which effectively gave all the integrated design elements a voice, not only for the building itself but also for the artificial intelligence housed within it.

☒ SUMMA, 2017

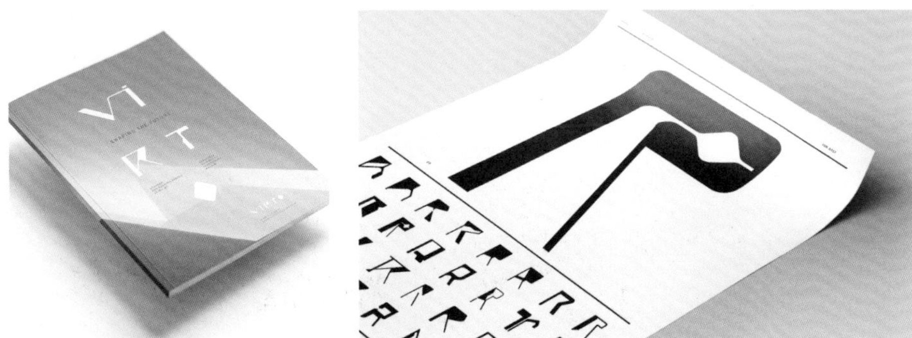

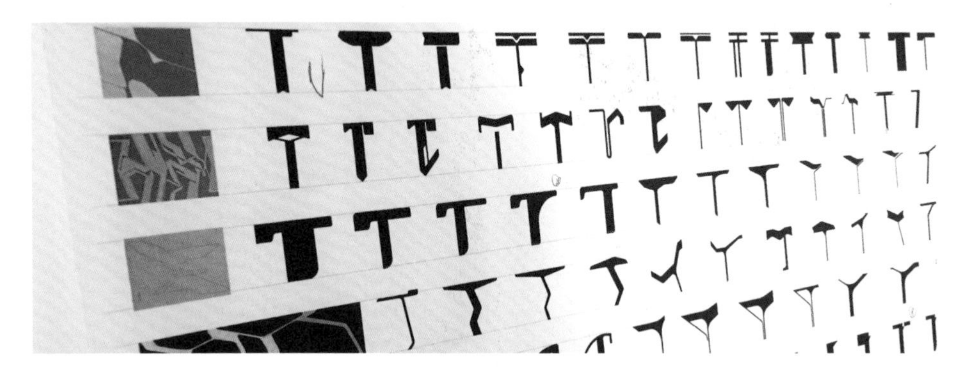

WIEN
MODE
RN29
ESSA
YS

WIEN
MODE
RN29
A–Z

WIEN
MODE
RN29
30. OKT BIS
30. NOV 2016

WIR?
UND
WO
ZUM
TEUFEL
SIND
WIR
HIER
UEBER
DER
N29
30. OKT
BIS
30. NOV
2016
ERSTE
BANK
KOMPO
SITIONS
PREIS
EINLA
DUNG
WIEN
MODE
RN29
PROG
RAMM
A–Z
ESSA
YS
30. OKT
BIS
30. NOV
2016
WWW. WIENMODERN. AT

WIEN
MODERN

MO
07
NO
V.
FR
18
NO
V.

Wien Modern
Typography in flux

Wien Modern is an annual music festival in Austria that was founded in 1988 by the Italian conductor Claudio Abbado to revitalize Vienna's traditional music scene. The festival features classical, avant garde and electronic music, as well as dance, performance and other forms of visual media. In 2016 the festival held 88 events at 21 venues across Vienna, exploring the theme of 'The Final Questions'. From the Vienna Philharmonic to audacious solo recitals, the London Jazz Composers Orchestra, pioneers of aleatory – or chance – music and a string of world premieres, this musical revitalization event is monumental. Wien Modern also presented a new identity and custom typeface in 2016, designed by the Pentagram Berlin team.

Pentagram completely reconceived Wien Modern's brand, keeping only the red as its identity touchstone. So, what served as the armature for the total identity is the inventive 'Wien Modern' monospace and monowidth typeface that was specially created for the festival – it featured on all digital and printed platforms, including posters, publications and more. Justus Oehler of Pentagram explains: 'In the festival's new monogram, the font creates geometric typographic patterns, which express the festival's exploration of modern music.' A monospaced/monowidth font (or fixed-width, or non-proportional, font) is a typeface or type family with characters that each occupy the same amount of horizontal space and so it does not conform to more frequently used variable-width fonts, where the letters occupy different widths.

Pentagram created a titling typeface that could be applied in a modular way – a monospace font that looks like an illustration but is legible at the same time. Instead of a fixed logo device, this logo is in flux – it is the name set in this new typeface, on a single line, on two lines, on three, four or even five lines, combined with other information. Says Oehler: 'This way every title or headline can be made into a full-page graphic image.'

☒ Pentagram Berlin (Justus Oehler), 2016

Restaurant du Cercle de la Voile de Neuchâtel

The sea without the cliché

When creating logos for fisheries, maritime-themed products and – especially – seafood restaurants, designers (and doubtless their clients too) assuredly rely on the standard stereotypes to telegraph their bills of fare and myriad offerings: fish, fishnets, shells, seagulls, flags, boats, life-preservers, mermaids and much more.

When Supero, a design agency based in La Chaux-de-Fonds and Neuchâtel, Switzerland, was commissioned to design the logo and menus for a sailing club's public restaurant, Restaurant du Cercle de la Voile de Neuchâtel, it wanted to avoid clichés related to the world of Neptune and suggest instead the maritime world in a subtle way through typography alone. Supero found the answer in the fortuitously numerous letters 'e' in the name. Although the waving 'E' arguably resembles a flowing pennant, it more overtly suggests the rolling waves of the sea.

Black and white are not typically seafaring colours, but that was deliberate. They did, however, use a sea blue for the placemat design (which is a single large 'E', suggesting the plates are floating in the water). The waves – which in this composition are different in each orientation of the 'E' – also serve as the branding statement for the club's special events posters and brochures. So simple and unpretentious, the wavy 'E' motif, while never a substitute for the longish name, has become an efficiently striking alternative when graphic shorthand is needed.

☒ Supero, 2016

« J'AI DÉPENSÉ 90%
DE MON ARGENT
EN ALCOOL ET EN
FEMMES. LE RESTE,
JE L'AI GÂCHÉ. »

GEORGE BEST

SANS CONTESTE LE MEILLEUR

CVN-RESTAURANT.CH

EURO 2016 SUR ÉCRAN
GÉANT. GRILLADES,
BINCHS ET HURLEMENTS !

CERCLE DE
LA VOILE DE
NEUCHÂTEL

Develop a memorable monogram

Crane & Co. / Obama / Volvo / Riot

Crane & Co.
Concentric complexity

For someone who loves to design monograms so much, New York-based designer Louise Fili continues to find them challenging. No matter what the initials are, she says, 'they always seem to be the wrong ones at the start of the design process'. However, when it is completed and the letters are 'cohabitating comfortably' the emblem betrays not the slightest hint of a struggle.

Crane & Co. is an eighth-generation New England paper company synonymous with fine materials and exquisite craftsmanship. It needed a monogram that could be implemented across many platforms, products and materials – from the website to stationery; on paper, cloth and metal. Moreover, the mark needed to embrace Crane's long history while at the same time representing its status as a progressive luxury brand. Fili recommended that their logotype would benefit from an overhaul: 'Why buy a new dress if you are going to wear it with the same old pair of shoes?'

The existing logotype, which was simply a horizontally scaled version of Trajan, had to be adjusted to work in conjunction with the monogram yet also stand on its own. In addition, she considered how the monogram could apply itself to a maker's mark – an iconic, abstracted version that could easily be recognized as the symbol of the brand.

Four treatments were presented. She offered them a choice of four initial combinations: capital 'C', ampersand, capital 'C', lower-case 'o'; capital 'C', capital 'C', lower-case 'o'; capital 'C', ampersand, capital 'C'; and capital 'C', capital 'C', ampersand. The Housatonic River, where the Crane mill is located, provided inspiration for the natural flow of the nesting 'C's and ampersand. Each of these options was shown with a corresponding logotype, none of which was radically different from the existing logo. 'But the perception of renewed elegance made all the difference', she said.

When Fili presented the monogram to Crane & Co., they had a difficult time arriving at a consensus. They had another meeting, this time at Fili's studio, where she 'threatened' them that no one could leave until a decision was reached. 'We held a secret ballot and', she said, brandishing the one shown here, 'they unanimously agreed.'

⊠ Louise Fili, 2015

Obama'08

Obama
Branding of a president

Barack Obama won two successive elections for the office of President of the United States; in both instances he also won the design race. His campaign understood that coordinated graphics were beneficial and modern typography could be used to signal *change* (which also was his campaign's motto). All those who are seeking elective office in the United States have long followed similar, mundane branding formats: traditional typefaces and combinations of red, white and blue, accented by a patriotic element like a star, stripe or American flag. The Obama 'O', the jewel in the crown of a synchronized design scheme, challenged the status quo, and it further represented the rising sun of a new day.

Sol Sender, the designer for the original 2008 logo, noted that there were seven or eight options in the first round, and the one that was ultimately chosen was among these originals. In terms of the project's internal process, the logo came out of a second round of design explorations quite quickly – the entire undertaking took less than two weeks.

The 'O' did not elect the candidate, but it did signal change. Only time will tell whether it altered the clichés that dominate election graphics, although more contemporary typefaces and soothing hues have appeared in recent election materials.

Many observers admired the sophisticated typography of the design scheme, particularly the eventual consistent use of Gotham (not utilized by Sender), designed by Tobias Frere-Jones, which amplified the brand. Branding political messages consistently is incredibly hard to do. As a result, the Obama campaign graphics stood out – and even now, out of office, it continues to be the paradigm of branding excellence.

Logos and typefaces alone do not add up to a successful graphics campaign, but they serve to frame the content. Addressing the public requires a mnemonic that will perpetuate the good feelings towards the brand, product, or in this case the candidate.

☒ Sol Sender, 2008

Volvo
Telegraphing legacy and pride

The car emblem is a distinctive breed of logo. Designed to speak on emotional and business levels, they are modern-day heraldic shields that represent the legacy, reputation and purpose of an automobile company or distinguish the status of a particular model, whether luxury, sport or touring. For owners who take pride in their vehicles, emblems are sacred.

The essentials of the Volvo logo have remained much the same since the company was founded in 1927. Anonymously designed, the Volvo name derives from the Latin verb *volvere*, to roll, describing movement. The name is also easy to pronounce and spell.

The mark itself – a silver circle with an arrow pointing diagonally upwards at the top right side – is the chemical symbol of iron. It also represents the shield and spear of Mars, the Roman god of war.

The symbolic references to heroes, power and strength are apt. The emblem signifies Sweden's robust iron industry. A diagonal stripe that crosses the radiator grille is also an essential part of the Volvo identity and was used on the first car in 1927, originally serving to keep the chrome emblem in place. Gradually it became merely a decorative element. Still today it effectively distinguishes, also from a distance, Volvo vehicles from vehicles of other brands.

Since 1927 the design of the Volvo Iron Mark has been updated and modernized from time to time to further reflect and emphasize their core values: quality, safety and environmental care. Today, it is not only used on the vehicles, but also as the main communication symbol in advertisements, brochures, stationery, Internet sites and on merchandise.

☒ Redesign by Stockholm
Design Lab, 2014

RIOT

Riot
Four powerful letters

Making custom letters is almost always a given when creating a wordmark. While it is acceptable to use existing typefaces, that's like picking a suit off the rack instead of going bespoke. Speaking of clothes, a fashion label relies on uniqueness for success, so its logo – particularly in a marketplace where clothing is purchased as much for the brand name as the quality of the garment – must set itself apart from the competition (even if it is trying to conform to a particular genre or style).

Neville Brody's design for the Riot sub-brand of Supreme is a startling fashion statement that uses the designer's penchant for Russian Constructivist design in a contemporary context. Building the contoured sans serif word into a diamond shape in white on black or white on red is a powerful visual fusion of geometry and asymmetrical design.

When creating something as ephemeral as a fashion brand the idea is to make the logo look timely but at the same time timeless. That means simplicity is a virtue and boldness is a necessity. This is also a function of scale. The word 'RIOT' fills the space like the word 'STOP' fills a sign. Brody has found the right balance between new and old, now and then.

☒ Neville Brody, 2014

Make a symbol carry the weight

Windows / Qatar / CVS Health / 23andMe

Windows
A metaphor for screens

In 2012 Paula Scher, a partner at Pentagram New York, designed a new logo for Microsoft's Windows 8 that was meant to be 'a complete re-imagination of the Windows operating system'. At the initial meeting, Scher asked a simple yet defining question, referring to the previous iterations of their waving coloured window boxes: 'Your name is Windows. Why are you a flag?'

It was accepted that it was a flag and that it no longer needed to be. The original logo had evolved in a time of lower-resolution graphics. The boxes, initially representing 'windows', turned into a waving flag, probably as a result of someone complaining that a plain box was too static and severe.

Pentagram's new identity brought the logo back to its nascent window intention. The name Windows was introduced as a metaphor for seeing into screens and systems – 'and a new view on technology'. The Windows 8 logo formulated the familiar four-colour symbol as a modern geometric shape. In brand-speak it also introduced a new perspective on the Microsoft brand that reflects Microsoft's Metro design language for its Windows 7 phones. This is a streamlining of what had been, compared with Apple, the more cumbersome graphic schemes that defined Microsoft products, graphics and user interfaces. Windows 8's design principles are influenced by the Swiss, or International Typographic, Style, with clean lines, shapes and typography, and bold, flat colours – the interface avoids anything three-dimensional that use gradients or effects.

The windows metaphor is apt, having become a somewhat generic term for interface screens on *all* personal computers. With the new logo, Scher and Microsoft sought to celebrate the idea of opening a window to the world. Moreover, the four-colour symbol is a modern geometric shape that signals that the Microsoft brand is aiming to be easier to use.

The perspective analogy works well, according to Sam Moreau, Microsoft's Principal Director of User Experience for Windows, 'because the whole point of Microsoft products is that they are tools for someone to achieve their goals from their own perspective'.

☒ Pentagram, New York
(Paula Scher), 2012

قطر
QATAR

قطر
QATAR

قطر
QATAR

قطر
QATAR

قطر
QATAR

قطر
QATAR

قطر
QATAR

قطر
QATAR
قطر
QATAR
قطر
QATAR

Qatar
Arabic as pattern

During the early 2000s the Western design world began to take a renewed interest in Arabic lettering and typography, which draws upon an esteemed calligraphic heritage. Lebanon-born, Netherlands-based Tarek Atrissi, who had developed an online community to showcase newly designed Arabic typefaces for public use, was one of the pioneers of this renaissance. In 2003 he received an unprecedented commission: to develop a brand language for an entire nation.

☒ Tarek Atrissi, 2003/04

The Qatar Tourism Authority wanted a graphic identity for the wealthy Arab country that could be used to promote Qatar to telegraph it regionally and internationally as an attractive destination. This design-based nation branding, the first of its kind in the Persian Gulf, consisted of designing a logo, full brand visual guidelines, printed promotional material, digital and website elements as well as an advertising campaign.

Far from an easy task. As Atrissi put it: 'Designing the identity of a country is probably one of the most challenging and unique projects a designer could face. … Can the entire culture and image of a nation be reduced into a visual identity system?'

The outcome Atrissi created was simple and modern, yet one that drew its inspiration from the rich calligraphic heritage of Arabic, which is filled with gracefully flowing scripts. The graphic identity was expressed to appeal both to the local community and to Westerners. The minimalist logo used an innovative calligraphic style of the Arabic word 'Qatar', underlined with the name Qatar in a classic Baskerville typeface. 'For the Arab reader, the logo was a visual signature of the country', he says. 'For the non-Arab reader, the calligraphic shape became abstract forms interpreted differently by people and linked to various visual associations.'

Showcased here is a small selection of the design work developed by Tarek Atrissi Design for the government of Qatar. The identity he developed is a case study in the field of nation branding. The project's minimalist graphic approach was a positive influence on large-scale governmental projects in the Arab world.

CVS Health
A heavy heart pumps up the brand

When CVS Caremark Corporation transitioned into CVS Health in 2016 it introduced a new logo with the tagline 'Health Is Everything'. Siegel+Gale, the New York-based branding and design firm responsible, described the logo as 'foundational to how CVS Health distinguishes its role in shaping the future of healthcare for people, businesses and communities'.

The image makeover followed a bold, industry-defining strategic announcement that CVS Caremark would become the first chain pharmacy to take cigarettes out of its 7,700 retail stores, potentially sacrificing nearly US$2 billion in annual sales. The elimination of tobacco products was the impetus for Siegel+Gale's fresh look and feel that was intended to unite for the first time the company's four business divisions of CVS/pharmacy, CVS/specialty, CVS/minuteclinic and CVS/caremark.

The word 'Caremark' was replaced with an iconic heart shape that was universally familiar to all age groups, locales and languages, but it was stylized and made personal to Caremark by taking the typical curvilinear symbol and making it more like a bold 'V'. 'Its core geometry was created using teardrop shapes', explained Siegel+Gale in their mission statement.

Siegel+Gale designed the 'CVS Health Heart' to be a flexible graphic element – one that could even act 'as a pointer or bracket to emphasize important information'. The thin slab serif 'Health' type is simple but effective. Additionally, a new variegated colour palette (red being the primary one but there are happier pastel greens, purples, yellows and blues too) complements a library of icons and illustrations, both for visual levity and to help simplify complex or abstract ideas.

Building from the mark, the brand's tagline – 'Leading with heart' – followed, expressing a caring tone throughout the narrative. The company's values reside in this heart in the same way that Milton Glaser's 'I♥NY' bespeaks positive attributes like integrity, caring, collaboration, innovation and accountability.

⊠ Siegel+Gale, 2014

CVSHealth

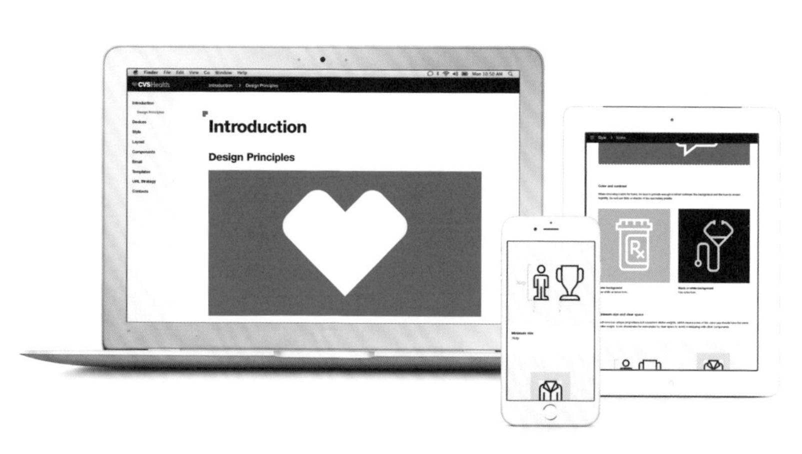
Introduction
Design Principles

SEPTEMBER 2014
C
CONNECTIONS
CVSHealth

Promise Kept
As of September 3, 2014, CVS/pharmacy is officially tobacco-free. Plan executed. Promise kept. One month ahead of schedule.

Our Tagline
Health is everything.

☒ MetaDesign, 2006

23andMe
The DNA of DNA logo

Personal genome profiling has become a popular, inexpensive procedure (like pregnancy testing) that offers untold medical data benefits. With popularity come services and products that require identity systems, and in the twenty-first century the rise of user-friendly industries, especially in the digital startup space, calls for an intimate or welcoming tone.

Into this new unthreatening healthcare arena in 2006 came 23andMe, a pioneer biotech company. Its logo was designed as a simple, colourful abstraction of the chromosomal tubular shape. The company takes its name from the 23 pairs of chromosomes into which human DNA is organized in every human cell – and from its founders' assertion that 'genetics is about to get personal'.

The international branding firm MetaDesign created the 23andMe logo. It is what the designers call a 'fluid' vector-based pictorial, with a transparent, overlapping colour system that changes both in hue and in orientation depending on the company's needs and services. The logo effectively synchronizes with 23andMe's promotional and packaging requirements.

But most importantly, for a company that is a service for average people looking to access such a complex and progressive area of science, the identity must overcome any sense of intimidation that many inherently feel in dealing with health issues. This logo has taken its lead from the Modernist pharmaceutical promotions of the late 1950s and 1960s, by mixing symbolic imagery and lively design elements.

Transform from one identity to another

BP / NASA / LEGO / Issey Miyake's L'Eau d'Issey / Jewish Film Festival

BP
From shield to sun

In 1997 British Petroleum's then CEO John Browne committed the oil giant to reducing its greenhouse gas emissions by 10 per cent by 2010. In 2000, following a series of mergers and acquisitions, BP decided to update and renew its corporate image of a traditional oil producer, transitioning from simply an oil and gas company to embrace new energy sources such as renewables.

The series of deals had made BP the largest oil company in the world at one point, although it was overtaken following the merger of Exxon and Mobil. Browne saw the opportunity to position BP's brand across all its businesses, including its investments in solar power, other alternative energies, and its partnerships with automakers to improved engine efficiency. Browne commissioned Landor to develop a new brand identity, and their sister company Ogilvy and Mather coined the slogan 'Beyond Petroleum' (using the initial letters 'B' and 'P').

BP's former shield mark was replaced with a stylized sunflower to symbolize the sun's energy to give the Helios identity. This retained BP's longstanding distinctive use of green, reflecting the brand's environmental sensitivity. The shift in identity telegraphed the message that BP was a provider of more than just oil and gas, but energy solutions. This proposition of a new environmentally friendly brand earned plaudits from some but triggered cynicism and criticism from others, notably green campaigners.

The brand champions (a network of 1,400 BP employees trained to market the narrative) used multiple media platforms to push the brand through custom toolkits that reinforced the Beyond Petroleum ethos. Landor even redesigned BP's physical environments, right down to the plants that became fixtures in many of its offices.

However, the Deepwater Horizon spill in 2010 subsequently forced BP to divest many of its alternative energy businesses as it raised funds to meet its obligations and pay compensation claims. This triggered a new brand driver – 'Providing energy in a better way' – which signalled a renewed emphasis on operational safety.

☒ Landor, 2000

NASA

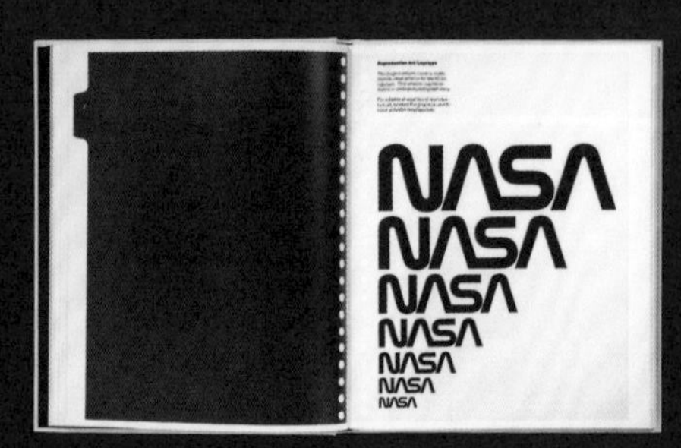
NASA
NASA
NASA
NASA
NASA
NASA
NASA

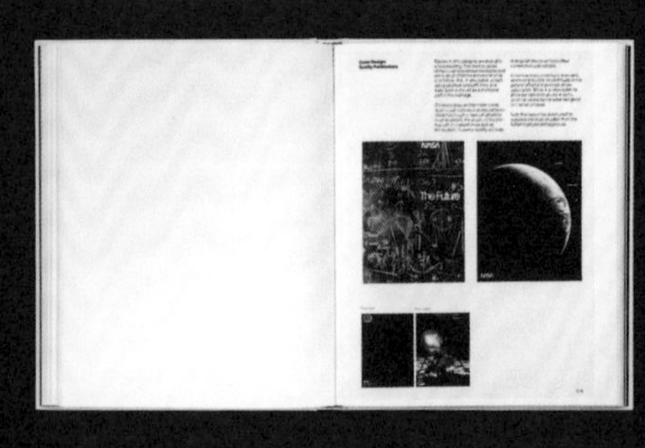

NASA

NASA

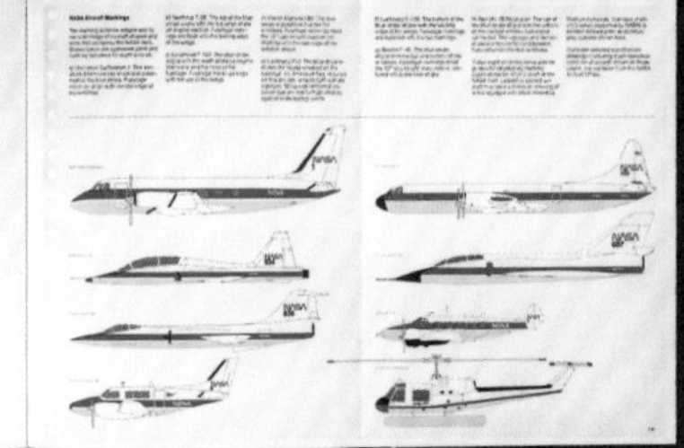

NASA
A wormhole into the future

The role of the National Aeronautics and Space Administration (NASA) when it was founded in 1958 was to be a forward-thrusting gateway to the future. As technology advanced, perceptions changed and NASA's graphic identity became prematurely obsolete. The first NASA logo was designed in 1959: a sphere representing a planet, stars representing space, a red chevron as a wing representing aeronautics and an orbiting spacecraft shooting around the wing. During the 1960s it served its trademark function well, yet by the 1970s it had lost its symbolic magic and, with it, the capacity to stimulate the imagination.

In 1973 the designers Richard Danne and Bruce Blackburn formed the corporate identity firm Danne & Blackburn, which was commissioned to work on a new NASA design programme to be built around a modern logo that typographically expressed optimism in NASA's prowess and science's power to conquer new worlds in outer space.

Launched eight years after the release of Stanley Kubrick's mind-bending film *2001: A Space Odyssey*, the NASA identity programme reflected the exactitude of scientific modernism and symbolized the promise of space age reality. 'We have adopted a new system of graphics', proudly wrote Richard H. Truly, NASA's administrator, in the new – now legendary – *National Aeronautics and Space Administration Graphic Standards Manual*, effective from 1 January 1976. He continued: 'The new system focuses on a new logotype, in which the letters "N-A-S-A" are reduced to their simplest form, replacing the red, white and blue circular emblem with the white block letters. I think the new logotype is pleasing to the eye and gives a feeling of unity, technological precision, thrust and orientation toward the future.'

☒ Danne & Blackburn, 1975

Known affectionately as 'the worm', the wordmark letters were serpentine and curvilinear yet not a novelty type – more like a vessel moving upwards and downwards through the emptiness of space. Graphically, the logotype was a new vision of the future. It wasn't a bitmapped computer cliché. When applied in multiple media, the unified system perfectly expressed the agency's growing confidence in its mission.

LEGO
Shape and colour that conjure the product

Few companies have gone through as many logo iterations as LEGO. It is a graphic tale of evolution, devolution and revolution, resulting in one of the most famous logos in the world.

In 1932 carpenter Ole Kirk Kristiansen started a modest shop in the village of Billund, Denmark, manufacturing stepladders, ironing boards, stools and wooden toys. By 1934 it had become a toy business called LEGO. Taking its original inspiration from the Danish *leg godt* ('play well'), the Latin *lego* means 'I put together'. Its woodcut-like trademark was used for letterheads, invoices and shipping labels, then in 1936 'LEGO Fabriken Billund' was imprinted on wooden toys. In 1948 LEGO began producing the interlocking blocks they are now famous for.

In 1954 the first of LEGO's oval logos appeared on LEGO Mursten ('bricks') catalogues. A year later the logo design and colour (bright red, yellow and white) was standardized for the first time and emblazoned on wood and plastic toys and packages. The logo features the word 'LEGO' spelled out in the original lettering, now known as LEGO Font. The letters are white, but are surrounded by thin borders of black and yellow and are set against a red, square background. The font of the logo is meant to be soft and light-hearted. Its rounded-edge, bubble shape conveys an idea of fun.

From 1960 to 1965 the first of the current square logos were activated and variants were used worldwide for the next 13 years. This introduced colour bars (red, yellow, blue, white and black) and was the first to include the registered trademark as part of the LEGO name.

In 1973, as LEGO began production in the United States, the logo was 'modernized' but retained the familiar colour scheme, and was given a more brick-like shape, to remind customers of LEGO's core product.

In 1998 the logo was tweaked into its current form, with some 'graphic tightening' to make the colours brighter and more visible on the Internet, as well as ensuring better visibility on the shelves. The draw of the logo is in its bold typography. For products marketed to children, startling display is necessary to grab their attention. The logo's bright colours and large size have helped to build one of the world's most successful companies.

☒ Designers unknown,
revised 1998

ISSEY MIYAKE

L'EAU D'ISSEY

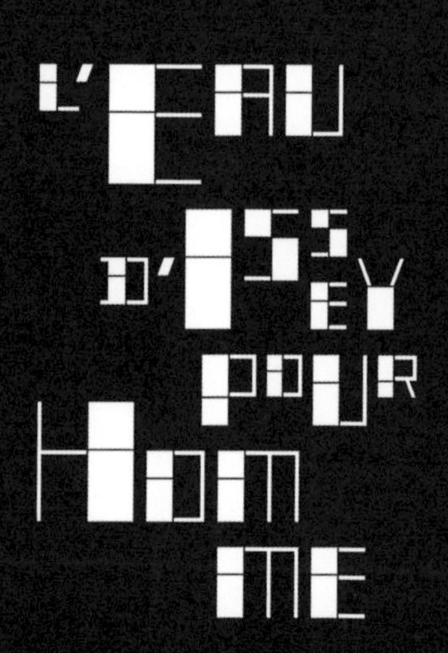

Issey Miyake's L'Eau d'Issey
Animated letters

It is no longer enough for a logo to be something static. A modern-day logo is usually used as part of a larger branding story, which could involve making the logo come alive through motion and music. This means that it is best if the logo is created in such a way that it is flexible enough to dance and sing.

French graphic designer Philippe Apeloig's stark black-and-white logo animation for Issey Miyake's L'Eau d'Issey embodies so many positive traits. It uses representative abstraction to convey a common perfume in a delightful manner that quickly transitions from shapes of the product to forms that create the logo itself.

Too often animated logos go to complicated extremes. The purity of this animated 'sketch' keeps the viewer watching, if only to see how the logo or brand name materializes. Apeloig has created something of a puzzle that the viewer enjoys seeing solved. This is the future of logo design: simple, kinetic, experiential – in short, a piece of animated performance art.

☒ Philippe Apeloig, 2017

Jewish Film Festival
CMYK combines to make impactful images

Process colours in printing (CMYK) have a functional role in reproducing full-colour or four-colour process images. CMYK refers to four inks: cyan (blue), magenta (red), yellow and key (representing black). But when used on their own or as mixtures they provide a uniquely contemporary yet curiously timeless effect too.

Logos that make use of overlapping primary colours have increased in number of late. But what they gain in luminescence when reproduced in colour they lose when translated into black and white. New York-based Bosnian designer Mirko Ilić's CMYK equality bars, which when combined echo the rainbow symbol for equality in sexual orientation, would not have the same impact if they were black and white or grey.

This mark, originally for a conference in Zagreb, naturally morphed by virtue of its colour and form into a vibrant symbol of equality across the racial and gender divides. It both figuratively and literally suggests the integration of different but entirely equal entities coming together as one. What's more, the mark would not work without all the elements: take away any colour and the message is lost.

⊠ Mirko Ilić, 2012

6. FESTIVAL ŽIDOVSKOG FILMA ZAGREB
FESTIVAL TOLERANCIJE, KINO EUROPA
20.-26.05.2012.
SVE FILMSKE PROJEKCIJE SU BESPLATNE, WWW.JFF-ZAGREB.HR
POD POKROVITELJSTVOM GRADA ZAGREBA
SPONZORI: MIRKO ILIĆ CORP., ATLANTIC GRUPA, ORBICO

T O L E R A N C I J A

T O L E R A N C E

6th ZAGREB JEWISH FILM FESTIVAL
FESTIVAL OF TOLERANCE, EUROPA CINEMA
20-26, May, 2012
ALL SCREENINGS ARE FREE OF CHARGE, WWW.JFF-ZAGREB.HR
UNDER THE PATRONAGE OF THE CITY OF ZAGREB
MEDIA SPONSORS: HRT, JUTARNJI LIST, OTVORENI RADIO, NET.HR, ZAREZ, CULTURENET.HR

Make a mnemonic

Campari / Le Diplomate / JackRabbit / Duquesa Suites

Campari
Bottle as indelible identity

There are many memorable two-dimensional printed marks and logos that are remembered as much for the objects on which they appear if not more than the type or image itself. The Victorian-era Coca-Cola script is unmistakable and has been so for well over 100 years. But the shape of the original bottle still announces the brand even if the print logo is absent. The same can be said about various other iconic products past and present, like Heinz Tomato Ketchup, the Rolls-Royce RR, and more.

When Italian Futurist designer Fortunato Depero designed the original cone bottle for Campari Soda he not only made a novel shape, he also laid the seeds for one of the most unique brand identities in the world. Depero's creation was a masterpiece of psychological manipulation that remains relevant in the twenty-first century. Despite the frequent refinements made to Campari's typographic logo, which even under Depero's tutelage was altered in major and minor ways to signal that the popular beverage responded to the changing times, the individual-sized bottle has remained consistent to this day.

The cone shape is not the only identifying component of this physical logo; the other is the bright red herb-infused alcoholic beverage that illuminates the otherwise clear glass. Campari Soda's distinctive shape and its characteristic coloured liquid combined with a distinguishing name in slightly differing typographic styles give the product its personality and heritage. It is a lesson for the designers of today, who rely on more than a simple mark to make an indelible mark.

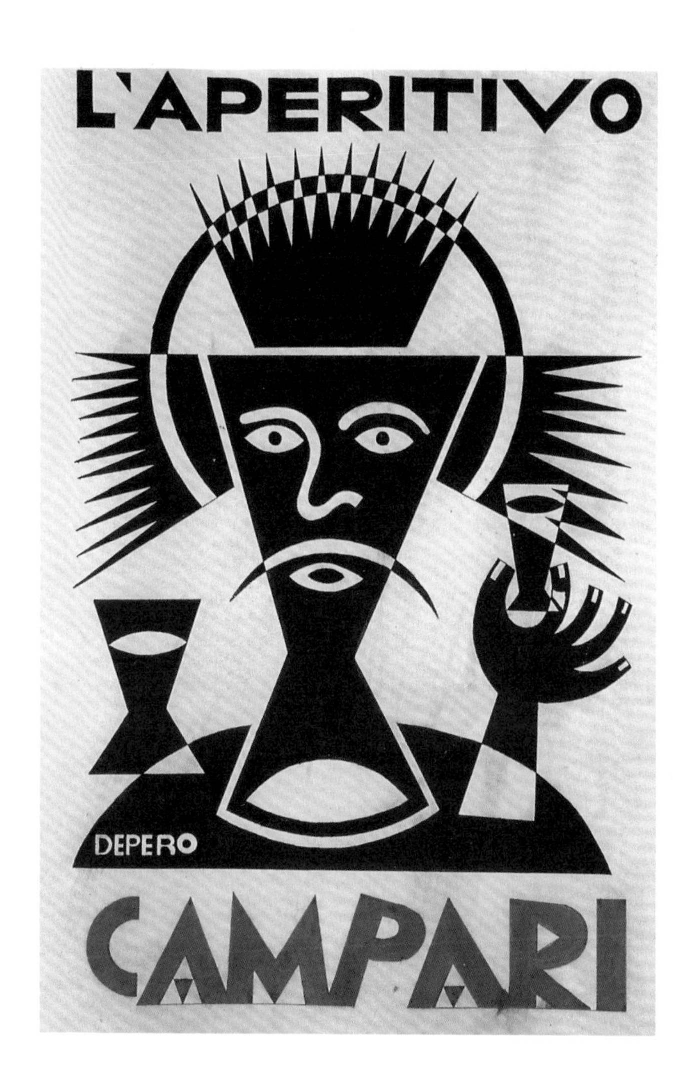

☒ Fortunato Depero, 1932

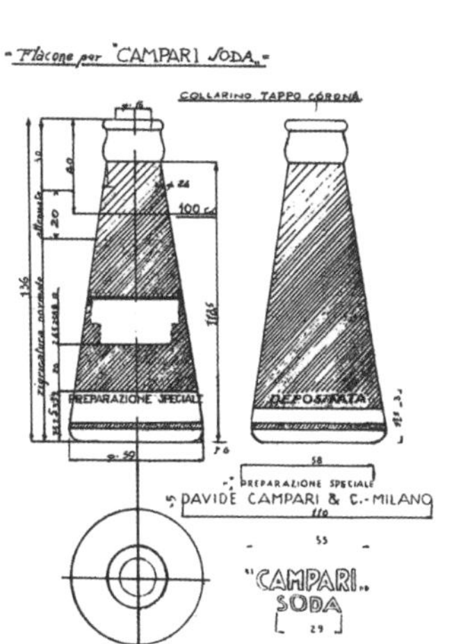

1601 14TH STREET, NW • WASHINGTON DC-20009
Le Diplomate
LEDIPLOMATEDC.COM • TELEPHONE: 202-332-3333

Carte des Vins
BREAKFAST: Coming Soon
BRUNCH: Sat & Sun: 10am-3pm
LUNCH: Coming Soon
Le Diplomate
EXECUTIVE CHEFS
BREAKFAST
Coming Soon
BRUNCH
DAILY AFTERNOON
Coming Soon
DINNER
Le Diplomate
APÉRITIFS • SPÉCIALITÉS • BISTRO • BAR À VINS
GENERAL MANAGER
WILLIAM WASHINGTON
Brunch
LES OEUFS

Le Diplomate
Design nostalgia as an escape

Restaurants that pay homage, through their graphic and interior design, to authentic French brasseries, bistros and cafés are extremely popular outside of France, if only to satisfy a certain wanderlust or nostalgia in their customers. These eating places are like theatre sets in which the diners are the actors. Designers also get genuine satisfaction from working with vintage typefaces and ornament, toying with an alluring pastiche of antique graphics yet creating something new. To get the customer enraptured requires a lot of detailed design.

Le Diplomate restaurant, created by Stephen Starr in Washington, DC, evokes the artful spirit of a Parisian brasserie, even down to the romantic brand language on its website: '… the interior and exterior pay subtle tribute to tradition, imbuing every meal with a sweeping sense of European drama.'

To make the past into the present, designer Roberto de Vicq was asked to draw upon his passion for a historical approach to the design. The inspiration for the logo was, he explained: 'Diplomacy and the typography of the early twentieth century. The German font Neue Schriften was designed in 1916, as diplomatic efforts were being made to keep the US out of World War I.' Le Diplomate serves espresso in cups adorned with the image of a dove bearing an olive branch, which is not only a symbol for peace but also pays tribute to Starr's favourite coffee La Colombe (French for dove). On the restaurant menu the wordmark sits in an intricately rendered, elegant border treatment offset by simple curlicues and sinuous lines.

Summing up the brand narrative, de Vicq says: 'In this French brasserie, the nitty-gritty and gridlock of Washington, DC, are checked at the door, and every problem can be solved by a fabulous meal.' To achieve this result graphically he used a variety of turn-of-the-century dingbats and ornaments. Yet there are typographic anomalies, insofar as some of the types and letters (including Little Cecily, Modesto and Sina) were designed more with a nod to the past than having been taken from the exact time.

⊠ Roberto de Vicq, 2014

JackRabbit
A squiggle suggests speed

Runners belong to a passionate community that has sporting brands hopping to keep them satisfied and well supplied. This market is usually brand loyal but it is fragmented, leading to various outlets for its products. Finish Line, a leading athletic shoe and apparel retailer, has been acquiring stores, including brand name franchises like JackRabbit Sports and New York Running Company. When Finish Line engaged Lippincott to rebrand them, they already owned 50 stores, with more in the offing.

A unifying brand was needed to tie together the various outlets across the country. Lippincott developed a five-year strategy to create a brand aimed at target customers while also engaging staff members to take pride in the stores' offerings. To be competitive in a crowded field, the new brand had to provide what, in brand-speak, is known as a 'differentiated retail experience, integrated across key digital and in-store touchpoints'; in other words, making a community of running enthusiasts feel their needs were being catered to in a novel manner.

The existing yellow-on-black JackRabbit Sports logo was too goofy and cartoony; it was felt to lack the sophistication needed to move the brand forward. The new mark was more abstract, fluid in form and suggested that the new rabbit was a smarter, more mature, linear rendering. When cropped and used as a backdrop in advertisements, it also suggested a racetrack. The new sans serif, rounded type was not as goofy as the earlier version and it evoked greater motion.

The research had pointed to the need to produce a message that would trigger the energy and fervour of the running community. The JackRabbit name already had its own brand equity but it could be evolved to appeal to new consumers. 'It hints at running without being explicit or limiting', notes Lippincott's mission statement. 'It is memorable, distinctive and evocative enough to support its customers' active lifestyles.' The word 'Sports' was removed, the type was changed and the new brand was off and running.

JackRabbit was launched during the 2015 New York City Marathon, heralding the brand's hoped-for lead position within the running community.

JackRabbit®

☒ Lippincott, 2016

DUQUESA SUITES
****

DUQUESA SUITES
BARCELONA
****
Plaça Antonio López 5
08002 Barcelona
TEL +34 937 379 125
info@duquesasuitesbarcelona.com
www.hotelduquesasuitesbarcelona.com

304

SI US PLAU,
NO MOLESTAR
POR FAVOR,
NO MOLESTAR
PLEASE
DO NOT DISTURB
DUQUESA SUITES

Duquesa Suites
Simplifying the commonplace

Logos are most effective when there is either a literal or, preferably, a symbolic relationship to the place, thing or idea that is represented. The transformation or 'logofication' of commonplace images or objects is a very accomplished way of making a mark that identifies the hotel without being overly literal.

When designer Jordi Duró and his team were commissioned to design the identity for Barcelona's Duquesa Suites, they took their cue from the hotel's location, which was between the city's Gothic quarter and the Mediterranean Sea. The intention was to link this geographical relationship using historical and contemporary means. Duró determined that the sea would be the starting point. But rather than exploit familiar clichés like boats, fish or waves, they took a more fundamental yet less-obvious approach: rope and the cinch knots that seamen have used since time immemorial.

But rope alone does not a logo make. Translating the concept of a knot was a matter of drawing a suggestive shape that could be used in various iterations as a distinctive mark. It also had to distinctively stand alone as well as be an accent near the typographic name Duquesa Suites. Given the mark is based on a knot, Duró's idea was to create a balanced intersecting linear shape that evoked the cinch but was not exactly a knot. It also had to be versatile enough to be used in printed and die-cut forms on signs, cards, menus and a very elaborate 'do not disturb' sign.

☒ Jordi Duró, 2016

Illustrate with wit and humour

Dubonnet / Brooklyn Children's Museum / Art UK / Art Works / Music Together / Amazon / ASME / Edition Unik / Ichibuns / Oslo City Bike

Dubonnet
Sequential poetry

The evocative Dubonnet Man character was conceived by French designer and artist Adolphe Jean Édouard-Marie Mouron (who used the pseudonym AM Cassandre). Both became celebrities: the character for his ubiquity and Cassandre because his Dubonnet work was among the most iconic of the Art Deco era. Among the most heralded of his posters was a triptych for Dubonnet, the popular French aperitif made from wine, herbs, spices and quinine; it was part of a series that developed the product's persona and its venerated tagline, the onomatopoeic 'Dubo, Dubon, Dubonnet'. If repetition is the key to memory, then this construction succeeded three times in one image.

The Dubonnet idea was considered more of an advertisement than a logo, but in fact it fits neatly into both categories and *was* the de facto identity. Like many distinctive trademarks the poetic versatility of 'Dubo, Dubon, Dubonnet' makes it a powerful promotion and brand mark too, where the typography tells a story. This rapid textual/visual cadence is appealing – indeed habit-forming – for its integral rhythmic syncopation. It is also no coincidence that Dubonnet includes *bon*, the French for 'good'.

The Dubonnet identity was the first of many memorable campaigns worked on through Cassandre's Paris-based collaborative studio Alliance Graphique. It was special, in part, because the witty mascot transforms in a symbolic manner as 'he' turns from a partially coloured sketch into a fully formed drinker as he consumes the product within the first two panels and refills his glass in the third. At the same time, the bold sans serif product name fills in with black (Dubo, Dubon, Dubonnet). In addition to the sophisticated verbal and graphic conceits that provide a one–two–three punch to the viewer, Cassandre used the art of humour to achieve the final result, a methodology called the 'play principle'. American designer Paul Rand (who, incidentally, continued the Dubonnet Man campaign, with Cassandre's blessing, when it was introduced to the United States market) defined this principle as 'coping with the problems of form and content, weighing relationships, establishing priorities' – and ultimately having fun.

⊠ AM Cassandre, 1932

DUBONNET
DUBONNET
DUBONNET

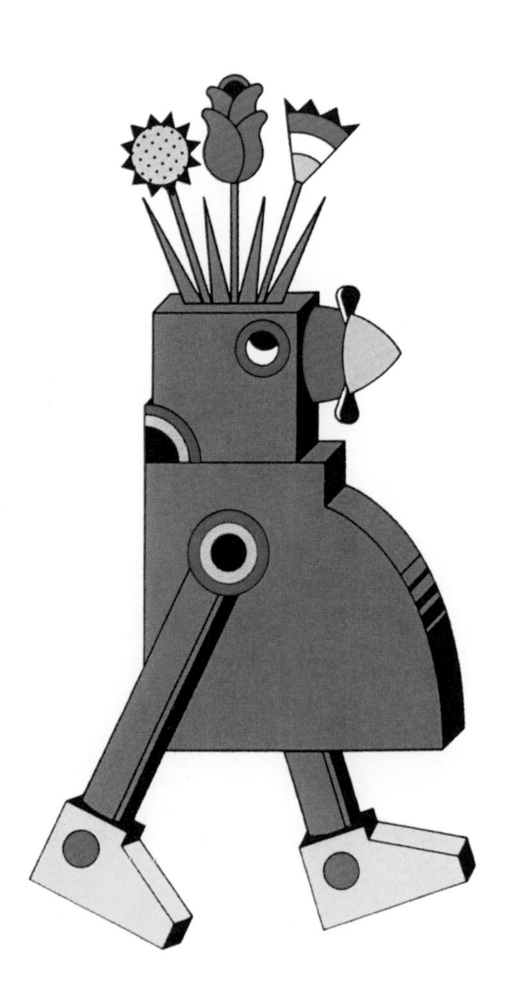

Brooklyn Children's Museum
Humanizing fantasy

To create an identity that would attract a parent and child audience to the Brooklyn Children's Museum, founded in 1899 as the world's first museum of its kind, demanded a character mark that was at once playful, distinctive and memorable, without being timebound, pandering or kitsch.

Seymour Chwast, co-founder of Push Pin Studios, was the right choice. With his singularly witty, joyful style, he had created over 30 children's books and designed dozens of character marks, as well as a fair number of word-type logos. For the Brooklyn Children's Museum he blended a mechanical, schematically composed rendering method with a delightful sense of cartoon absurdity.

The mark is a robot with an anthropomorphized charming demeanour. It suggests movement – an abundant attribute of the museum, where visitors interact with the exhibits – and imagination, which is the hallmark of all children's education. Chwast gives the robot personality by combining animate and inanimate forms. The bird-like bill is a propeller (one can imagine it spinning); the legs are rods attached to a colourful join, with footwear suggestive of high-top sneakers. The also bird-like eye is on the side of the square head, looking upwards at a plume made of flowers.

The rendering exudes a kind of postmodern decorative aura, but that trait does not lock it into a rigid stylistic time period. Still in use more than four decades after it was designed, the logo has a life of its own. It also has a unique advantage: it predates the current popular obsession with all things robotic, but postdates the clunky clichéd robots of the 1950s. It has a handmade quality, but also dips into the technological future.

⊠ Seymour Chwast, 1975

ARTUK
Members
ARTUK
Members

ARTUK

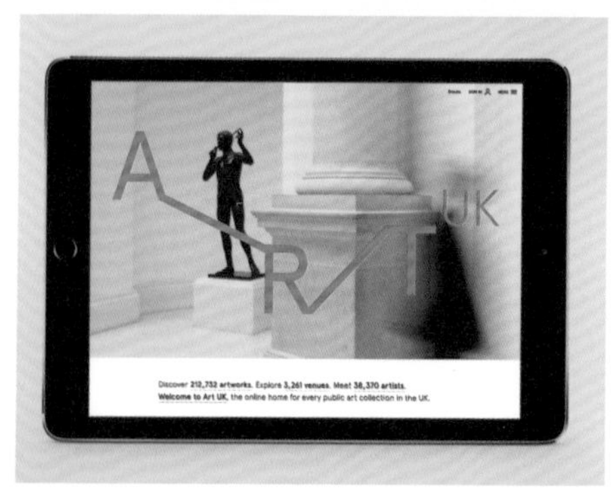
ARTUK
Discover 212,732 artworks. Explore 3,261 venues. Meet 38,370 artists.
Welcome to Art UK, the online home for every public art collection in the UK.

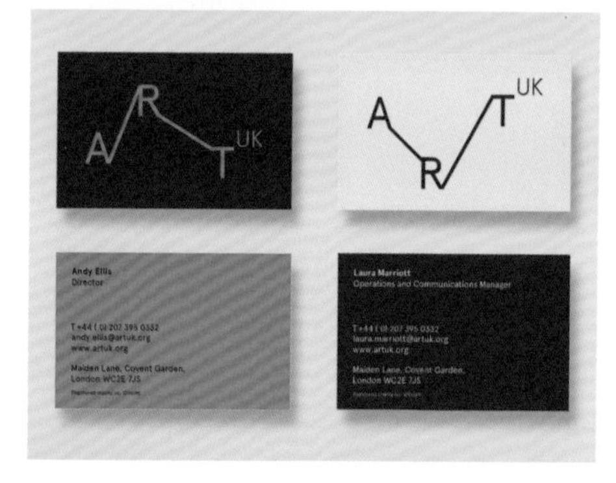
ARTUK
ARTUK
Andy Ellis
Director
T +44 (0) 207 395 0332
andy.ellis@artuk.org
www.artuk.org
Maiden Lane, Covent Garden,
London WC2E 7JS
Laura Marriott
Operations and Communications Manager
T +44 (0) 207 395 0332
laura.marriott@artuk.org
www.artuk.org
Maiden Lane, Covent Garden,
London WC2E 7JS

Art UK
Lines of communication

The word 'art' has been logofied in countless ways. Like art itself, a logo featuring the word must be beyond unique and still link to the audience.

Art UK is an online showcase for all the art owned by the United Kingdom in all of its public collections. The UK has the world's greatest public art collection, with 212,732 artworks by 38,370 artists displayed throughout 3,261 venues in England, Scotland and Wales. Art UK is digitizing many of Britain's treasured and lesser-known works to provide availability in one comprehensive virtual collection and it is summed up by the tagline: 'Welcome to the Nation's Art.'

Marina Willer and Naresh Ramchandani at Pentagram London designed the new logo in 2016. The capital letters 'A', 'R' and 'T' are linked together with equal weight lines to express the theme of connectivity. 'It is flexible and elastic, indicating different points of access and ways of interpreting art', the designers explain. That each letter of the logotype is joined to another reflects how the public interacts with the Art UK website and the artworks that can be accessed.

The mark has various permutations – the letters can be randomly positioned up or down as long as the lighter-weight type for 'UK' is always in the same close proximity to the capital letter 'T'. The various colours used further reflect the wide range of art on the website. Pentagram also coined the name to signify the organization's change of strategy and its shift away from printed catalogues to the current digitized collection (until then it was called the Public Catalogue Foundation).

After Pentagram worked with Art UK to define its brand, another key component developed on all digital and print platforms is photographs of art in situ showing engaged visitors. The logo's physical and metaphorical elasticity allows it to be applied across any of Art UK's images.

⊠ Pentagram, London (Marina Willer), 2016

Art Works
The typovisual pun

Sometimes an idea for a logo fits so perfectly, springs forth so instantly and is so essential to the perception of what it represents that there is no other alternative. This is true for the mark for Art Works, a non-profit National Endowment for the Arts educational programme. Designer Nathan Garland says that 'the idea revealed itself in an instant' once the problem was defined. 'Several quick sketches enabled me to "save" what I envisioned.' However, developing the design meant exploring many possibilities.

The idea has an elegant, literal simplicity. 'I wanted the logo to show and tell its story as a compact still life', Garland explains. The logo depicts an easel formed by a capital 'A', that supports the words 'Art Works' and represents a symbolic painting or picture. The focal point, the two-word phrase, was specified by the NEA. It can be read in two meaningful ways: as a noun that represents what artists make or as a sentence composed of a noun and a verb that represents the artist's process *or* someone's experience of art. (The lower part of the easel can also be seen as the legs of a dancer, suggesting the performing arts.)

There were no other conceptual options. But many variations and refinements were generated in order to find the best way to configure and resolve the logo's overall form and typography.

What makes this a unique answer to the problem is its duality. It is fresh yet familiar, and it intends to evoke surprise, interest and clarity. The logo achieves what Paul Rand famously said was to 'defamiliarize the ordinary' or tweak an appropriate cliché so that it becomes something else, something new.

Art Works

☒ Athletics, 2016

Music Together
Little marks make loud sounds

The most important lesson to be learned from Music Together is that simple forms and subtle marks can be as impressive and loud as bold ones. Music Together is an early childhood music and movement development programme offering classes for children up to eight years old. It is a franchise with licensees offering the programme around the world. Any company that serves children must direct their brand to young parents, so when asked to develop Music Together's new identity, the Brooklyn-based firm Athletics ensured that the design elements expressed a level of sophistication while at the same time being modern and playful.

The identity is based on minimalist shapes and soothing colours. The graphic forms are inspired by musical notation – from Music Together's signature song 'Hello, Everybody!' in particular. The lower-case 'g' is the key character (as both the letterform and personality), using a curved line as the descender of the 'g', which also hints at the proverbial smile. The wordmark was extended into a full alphabet, which is used for display type as well as Music Together programmes and sub-brands so that everything hangs together.

Athletics note that the curve or 'arc' from the 'g' 'became a connector and activator for the brand language, which was set up as a tie-in to the logo' – as in 'Make Beautiful – Music Together' and 'Bounce with – Music Together'. The music-inspired shapes become additional graphical elements for the system, reinforcing the feeling of playfulness and musicality. These shapes also evolved into 'Friends', a set of dynamic, animated characters. By personifying the shapes, the Friends can be globally representative and comprehensive without the need for gendered or cultural identifiers.

The photography used throughout the brand features real Music Together families and it contrasts with the minimalist marks. All were shot on a white seamless background so it could be replicated easily and is usable in a variety of settings.

Amazon
The corporate happy face

Amazon.com is a staple of the new digital economy. But the company's trademark was not always the unmistakable corporate happy face that appears today.

In 1994 Amazon's founder Jeff Bezos conceived an idea for an online bookstore. Originally he called it 'Cadabra' (as in Abracadabra), but the name was mistaken for 'cadaver'. Realizing the confusion, Bezos decided the name should start with an 'A' and perhaps have a 'Z' to represent the range of books for sale. The result was Amazon – the largest river in the world representing what was intended to be the largest bookstore in the world. The original iterations included an 'A' with a serpentine shape, suggesting a river running through it. That did not last long. During the late 1990s some unmemorable typographic corporate-style wordmarks were attempted. In 1999 Bezos expanded the reach of the company by making it a total shopping experience. By 2000 the current lower-case sans serif Amazon.com type was introduced, but something was still missing.

Enter the design firm Turner Duckworth, which added a swooping yellow arrow that points from the letter 'a' to the 'z'. The round-edged, fluidity with the upturned bend at the bottom stem of the 'z' implies a smile to symbolize a sense of human satisfaction with the consumer experience whenever an Amazon package arrives.

The typography is bold and the total mark radiates visual wit. Emerging from the type, the swooping line is an enjoyable accent (akin to the bow on the UPS logo designed by Paul Rand). The designers note: 'Visual wit isn't about making jokes – it's about bringing warmth and humanity through design. It takes a light touch and the ability to see connections where others don't.' In fact, the smile is so effective that it is familiar to the public even when the company name is omitted in favour of an initial. Perhaps Bezos said it best: 'Anyone who doesn't like this logo doesn't like puppies.'

☒ Turner Duckworth, 2000

ASME
American Society of Magazine Editors

ASME
Blue edit marks make a mark

ASME is the American Society of Magazine Editors, and once the tagline is read the cleverness behind using editing marks is as clear as a clean galley of type. The logo, by Fred Woodward, recalls old school editing, when corrections were written on paper.

When, over 20 years ago, Woodward designed the logo he recalls: 'I missed holding a dog-eared manuscript in my hand ... [the] cheap, thin paper that had been banged out so hard on a manual typewriter that it felt like de-bossed Braille, so saturated with the editor's (and copy-editor's) non-repro blue corrections that it resembled hieroglyphics. By the time a story made it through the gauntlet of the editing process there was often as much blue on the page as black ... a bruising experience for any writer's ego.' That experience was the spark for this mark.

The first iteration was a typewriter-version of the same idea, pounded out on a little vintage Olivetti portable. It was quickly deemed too retro for a forward-looking organization. The revised (and final) version used a then newish cut of Bodoni with which, Woodward adds, 'I had recently fallen in love (as I was prone to do) ... Looking at it now, I must have been especially smitten with the dingbats, perhaps too much so; if I were given the chance to do it all over again, well, I might lose those brackets.'

A few years ago, he was asked to create a video introduction to ASME's National Magazine Awards ceremony. He needed something to get a drinking crowd's attention, so he added a preamble: a brief-but-LOUD macro video of the letters *A-S-M-E* being hammered, like gunshots, by typewriter keys deeply into the pulp bearing the editor's mark-up, handwritten with that squeaky non-repro blue felt-tip, and transforming four random characters into the logo. Now *both* Bodoni and typewriter versions of the logo remain in use today.

☒ Fred Woodward, 2000

Edition Unik
A logo that will never forget

Making faces out of typefaces is easy but making entire animals from letters is considerably harder to do, unless the right typeface is selected for the right word. For example, at first sight the deceptive logo for the Zürich-based Edition Unik, a programme that helps the elderly draft and publish their memories in a printed book format, is fairly enigmatic. The word itself, set in Warnock Pro type, reads as 'unik' with an additional graphic element emerging from the ascender of the 'k' that is likely to confuse the unprepared viewer. However, once the mark is considered for a few more seconds, the viewer will see a surprising non-type image materialize.

It is particularly clever that the logo for this project, which is devoted to preserving the elderly user's earliest memories, transforms into the depiction of that member of the animal kingdom that legend has it 'never forgets' – an elephant. This simple concept was smartly conceived by Raffinerie AG für Gestaltung, Zürich, a leading editorial agency based in Switzerland that for over 17 years has been developing a portfolio of typographic marks and pictorial logos.

The Warnock Pro works perfectly in this context. Although it is a modest face, it nonetheless exudes a decidedly contemporary aesthetic, which is good. Yet more important still is the serif of the lowercase 'k', which is a perfect elephant's trunk, and the dot of the 'i', which is conveniently positioned as its eye. It's a logo the viewer will never forget.

☒ Raffinerie, 2016

ICHIBUNS

イチバンズ

Ichibuns
Hypnotic allure

Sometimes a logo is a composite of elements designed to trigger Pavlovian responses. Ichibuns, a new Japanese-inspired dining concept in London's Soho district, is distinguished by two things: the quality of the menu available, which on the surface has similar offerings to many other Japanese restaurants; and its frenetic Ginza-esque graphic identity. For the food, of course, eating is the test, whereas the visual identity can be assessed from further afield and its vibrancy and graphic play is seductive.

Spinach, a London-based brand and communications agency, created the Ichibuns brand over an 18-month period. The agency was contacted by Paul Sarlas, a respected entrepreneur in the restaurant business, who told Leigh Banks, Spinach's Director of Branding, about a new *wagyu* (*wagyu* refers to Japanese-bred beef that provides high amounts of unsaturated fat) burger bar concept they wanted to create, and asked whether Spinach would be interested in pitching for the work. The man who conceived the Ichibuns concept was Robin Leigh. He had recently visited Hokkaido, Japan, and been inspired by the landscape, the tasty dishes and their natural ingredients. This exposure triggered his idea of creating a *wagyu* burger experience that used the best of Japanese produce and was set in a unique and vibrant burger bar atmosphere born out of the Shōwa period (corresponding to the reign of Emperor Hirohito from 1926 to 1989). Robin Leigh's brief was 'to create a unique and untouchable brand'.

The circular logo with Japanese characters and linear ornamentation is just one piece of a larger visual overload experience, along with the Japanese street food phenomenon itself. Incidentally, the Japanese text in the logo translates as 'Ichibuns'.

☒ Spinach Design, 2017

Oslo City Bike
The face tells the story

New logos are fast cropping up in business arenas such as urban bike-sharing services, which continue to surge. Some of the logos are linked to sponsors, like Citibank in New York City, which uses the equity of its existing logo to identify and popularize the bank. Others are like Oslo City Bike, a sharing service sponsored by Urban Infrastructure Partner, owner and operator on behalf of Clear Channel Norway. Oslo City Bike has a separate and distinctly witty brand mark that underscores an overall visual strategy: 'Working with multiple interdisciplinary teams, we've developed an engaging and lighthearted way of presenting the city bike.'

Oslo City Bike's logo is a visual pun – a quirky smiley-face abstraction of a bike with the seat and handlebars used as eyelids while tyres form the eyes. The overall character and personality is based on a series of excerpted parts, where the mark shifts eye movement as different aspects of the service are engaged. The graphic language comes to life through interactions that inform the user of such things as slippery roads, technical problems and updates in service.

For the sharing model to be efficient, the 'mantra' of Oslo-based design agency Heydays has been that the whole identity should be an integral part of it: 'In every respect it should leverage, simplify and clarify functionality and communication.' The brand, hardware, application and staff are therefore considered 'parts of a cohesive whole'.

The brand identity's goal – centred on the friendly logo – was to create excitement and ease. Heydays' mission is to keep things simple, which is achieved through logo, interface and the ultimate accessibility of the system.

The mark and its website graphics and app, Heydays insists, have engaged people around a shared, public service. 'Together with the launch of the redesigned bike, additional bikes in circulation, the new app, and many other improvements, the new identity boosted the number of trips taken per bike by 140% (to a total of well over 2 million trips each year). This puts Oslo citizens among the top of the world's most active city bicyclists.'

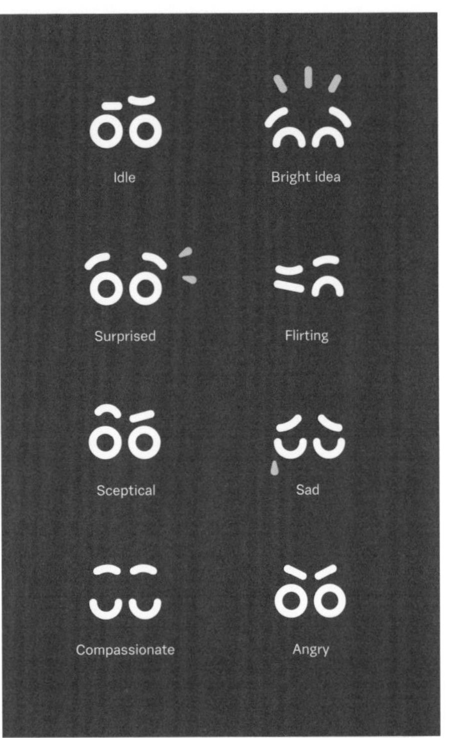

☒ Heydays, 2016

Include secret signs

Solidarity / FedEx / 1968 Mexico Olympics / Telemundo / Nourish / PJAIT

Solidarity
Letters on the march

In 1980 the Polish word 'SOLIDARNOŚĆ' ('solidarity') represented an end of 35 years of Soviet influence and domination of a once-independent nation. The word became a logo and the logo was not only a banner of the Polish revolution, but also a signpost for other nations similarly imprisoned behind the Iron Curtain.

The Solidarity mark, designed to suggest a parading mass of individuals united in a common cause, was designed by Jerzy Janiszewski, a graphic artist living in Gdansk. The city was known for the mammoth Lenin Shipyards, where the first signs of popular protest against the communist regime had emerged and flourished. Within a month of the mark's first appearance, it had become the ubiquitous emblem of the Polish national worker's movement. As a result of rigid censorship, this mark of an illegal labour union was banned, but it was not crushed and continued to speak as a symbol of popular revolt.

The Solidarity independent labour movement arose when the strike at the shipyard expanded to include workers of all kinds and students throughout Poland. Solidarity was a grassroots movement that was low on resources but high on energy. Paper and ink were scarce: what little could be foraged was quickly used on posters and bills, wheat-pasted onto public walls, and seen throughout the world. Poland was ripe for change and the scrawled logo embodied the essential power of the disaffected masses. Poland had a tortured past of Catholicism and nationalism 'blended into a synchronous passion', Lawrence Weschler wrote in *Virginia Quarterly Review*. The country had also lived through many failed national rebellions. Printed in red on white, the colours of the Polish flag, this historic mark represented much more than labour unrest – it was an expansive movement for social justice.

The Solidarity movement gave rise to many quickly produced graphic images – echoing the graphics of the Paris student and worker uprising in 1968 – but none was as powerful as this visual expression of protesting men and women that focused the eyes and ears of the world on SOLIDARNOŚĆ and the challenge to tyranny that it represented at that time.

⊠ Jerzy Janiszewski, 1980

FedEx®

FedEx
Pointing to a surprise

Hidden messages in logos are sometimes more overt than not. When the FedEx logo was redesigned in 1994, by Lindon Leader at Landor Associates, it seemed to be a straightforward refresh rendered as an abbreviation. Then, as the logo received wider attention, the public started murmuring about seeing an arrow in the negative space between the 'E' and the 'x'. This alluded primarily to FedEx's ability to move letters, packages and freight from point A to point B and with 'speed and precision'.

☒ Lindon Leader/Landor Associates, 1994

Originally the logo was a dark purple and red-orange wordmark that spelled out the name, suggesting an association to the US Postal Service. Customers had shortened it to 'FedEx' but didn't realize it was an international service. The CEO called for a brand change. The primary requisite was to make the trucks serve as moving billboards and spread the word.

The gamut of designs was tried. 'We knew we had to respect the brand cachet but extract the real value, make key decisions on what to keep, what to delete, what was usable, and what wasn't', Leader told *Fast Company* magazine. 'For example, we knew we wanted to keep the orange and purple – it was recognizable, so we wanted to exploit that – but make the orange less red and the purple less blue.'

Two typefaces were considered, Univers 67 and Futura Bold, set extremely wide and locked together, in upper case and lower case. In one iteration Leader took a capital 'E' and a lower-case 'x' and squeezed the letter spacing: 'I saw a white arrow start to appear between the "E" and the "x"', he said about tweaking the high 'x' of Univers and mixing it with the stroke of Futura Bold. The 'x' rose to the crossbar of a lowered 'E' 'and eventually not only did the arrow look natural and unforced, but I ended up with a whole new letterform'.

There was, purposely, no mention of the hidden arrow when the logo options were presented. 'Our goal was to not reveal it, to see if it got discovered.' Once the arrow was out of the bag, it became buzzworthy, Leader told *Fast Company* – it was necessary that PR not ruin the surprise. For those few who see it for the first time, it is still a revelation.

1968 Mexico Olympics
Optical illusions

The 1968 Olympic Games was the first to be hosted in a Spanish-speaking nation. For Mexico City it was an opportunity to show off the city for being as worthy as any of the world's capitals – London, Berlin, Rome or Tokyo – to host such a prestigious event.

Among the positive results of the 1968 Games (which was fraught with political unrest and controversy) was an ecstatic graphic design identity system centred on a wildly distinctive logo, and including all manner of posters, wayfinding and promotional graphics. The organizers had wanted to create a visual identity to tie together everything that was occurring during the Games, and they further hoped that the identity would help to 'sell' Mexico City to first-time visitors. This translated into developing a logo with a new look that was cosmopolitan and contemporary, and also distinctly Mexican. A competition to conceive the logo was awarded to Lance Wyman, then a 29-year-old graphic designer from New York City, and his design partner Peter Murdoch. In bridging both eclectic and modern styles, the result is one of the most phenomenal graphic brands in Olympic history.

Their research began with lengthy trips to the National Museum of Anthropology, where they studied artefacts from pre-Columbian Mexico, including the Aztec Sun Stone and ancient Mayan murals. 'I actually was floored by some of the early cultures,' says Wyman, 'because they were doing things that we were doing in a contemporary way with geometry and with graphics.' The bold lines and bright colours and geometric shapes reminded Wyman of the kind of Op art that was popular among contemporary artists back in New York, notably derived from MoMA's 1965 'Responsive Eye' exhibition, which featured dazzling Op art works. This and the pre-Hispanic indigenous Mayan art contributed to what Michael Bierut, writing in 1994 on the website Design Observer, called 'a geometric fantasia of concentric stripe patterns that expanded into a custom alphabet, groovy minidresses, and eventually entire stadia'.

Ironically, the designs would also be co-opted by local activists, who wanted to reveal the darker reality in Mexico – a reality that they felt was being covered up behind the glossy imagery of the 1968 Olympic Games.

☒ Lance Wyman, 1966

TELEMUNDO
IDENTITY
TELEMUNDO
TELEMUNDO

Telemundo
Window on the world

In the world of television, logos are imprinted on a viewer's brain like no other ubiquitous brand. Telemundo is the second-largest Spanish-language television network in the United States (now affiliated with NBC, with stations that can be seen throughout the USA and Latin America), after the market-leader Univision.

Telemundo had launched in Puerto Rico in 1954 and used a variety of logos before its major brand redesign in 1992. By then it required a mark that would adapt to its increasing media assets and could represent its expanding reach as it began to play a larger role on the world's telecommunications stage.

The original Telemundo mark was a red-striped globe, which, as designer Steff Geissbühler says, was too similar to other media companies for a network that was expanding so rapidly. 'The challenge was to create a strong, simple mark to be used everywhere: on air, in print, in advertising, and on microphones, trucks and satellite dishes', he explains.

The symbol that Geissbühler designed (when he was a partner at New York-based Chermayeff & Geismar) was a literal and symbolic language. It comprised a T-shaped viewing window ('tele') with a three-dimensional globe behind ('mundo').

The layered symbol sharply projects the illusion of a printed die-cut or 3D animation. The window further allowed for a litany of other symbolic images that introduced themes. On-air identifications were created, along with programme openings and closings. Graphic standards guidelines were developed for all applications. Although Geissbühler's approach was discontinued in 2000, the 'tele' T has remained the primary icon.

☒ Steff Geissbühler, 1992

Nourish
A carnival of healthiness

Nourish Snacks is a food company founded by TV celebrity nutritionist Joy Bauer. The company had strong early success with its granola treats, which had taken a chunk of that customer segment. Yet the product had been sold primarily online, so when it went from virtual to physical and had to compete on grocery store shelves, fighting for attention with dozens of other established brands, the challenge was to differentiate Nourish from the pack. The product's founders aspired to become a stronger challenger for snack lovers, which meant a refresh that encompassed all its graphic design assets. New York-based COLLINS was commissioned to develop a new strategy and an overhaul of Nourish's logo, packaging and digital presence.

Most snack-food packaging follows the same cliché of slapping a huge logo on the front along with a tasty photograph of the food. That is what Nourish did when it launched in 2014. For this rebrand COLLINS turned the tried-and-true standard on its ear in favour of what *Adweek* called: 'a design that looks like a melding of carnival signage with a 1970s TV game-show set, heavy on the browns and oranges, with the letters spelling "Nourish" each sitting in a circle floating above a field of stripes.'

The circus-inspired barber's pole diagonals and jittery type on the front of the Nourish package are reminiscent of the not-so-nourishing popcorn, peanuts and cotton candy – the usual midway fare. But the graphic excitement, which implies a sense of fun and delight, was worth the risk that customers might be disappointed. Brian Collins says that the 'whimsical language' of snacking – like cotton candy and ice cream cones – holds the promise of delight. But COLLINS didn't do its work in a vacuum: to best understand what, in the health-conscious twenty-first century, drives people into snacking, the company used ethnographic research, in-home and shop-along trips with customers, as well as interviews with key company stakeholders and retailers. Nourish Snacks are now sold at more leading retailers than ever before across North America.

☒ COLLINS, 2018

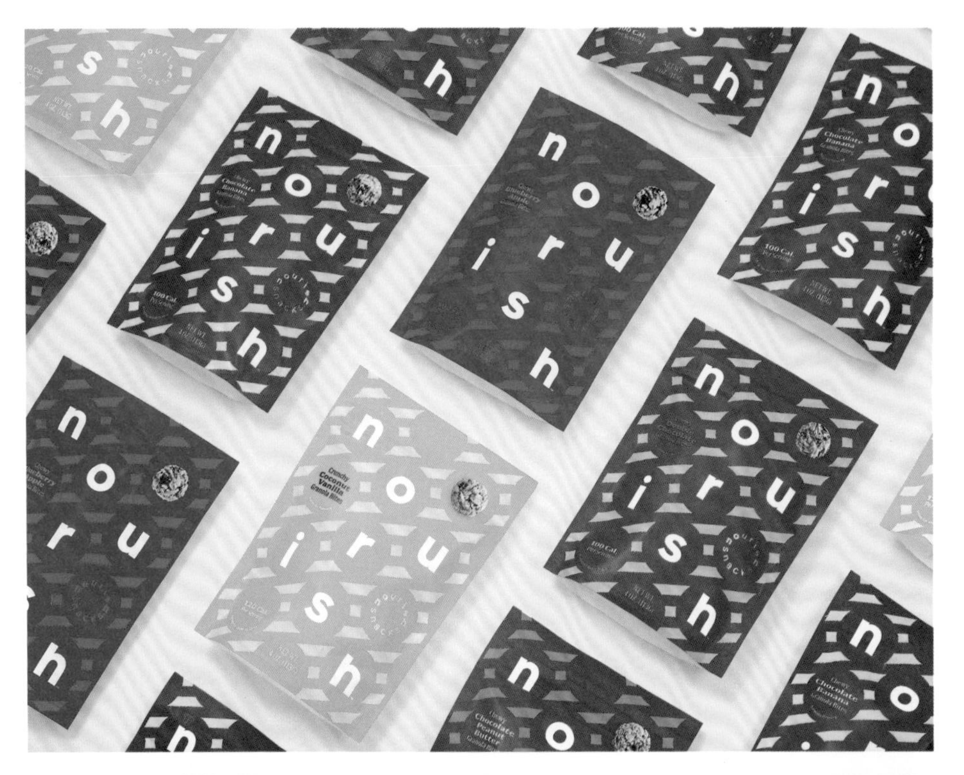
Chewy Chocolate Banana
Crunchy Coconut Vanilla Granola Bites
Chewy Chocolate Peanut Butter
100 Cal

Chewy Chocolate Peanut Butter
Chewy Chocolate Banana
12

PJAIT
Two flags and a happy coincidence

The Polish–Japanese Academy of Information Technology (PJAIT), founded in 1994, may seem like an odd pairing of national schools and educational cultures, but thanks to the Internet and the scores of digital platforms available the global village is growing larger. What's more, these two nations have an even more fundamental design component in common: their respective flags each feature red and white. This combination bestows its striking graphic language on the logo for PJAIT (or PJATK in Polish).

The flag of Poland consists of two horizontal stripes of equal width, the upper one white and the lower one red. The flag of Japan, known as the 'sun mark', is a rectangular white banner with a crimson disc at its centre. The logo for PJAIT is a round red disc with a white, slightly smaller, half-disc set within the top half of the red that suggests in one image the two nations – it is the perfect and simplest design solution possible.

The logo was designed for the PJAIT by the team at Zafryki (the studio that includes Piotr Młodożeniec and Marek Sobczyk). The mark began as a typical identity exploration, where the designers played with the concept of a red dot. 'In a short time, maybe one or two days, [we] noticed that one could divide the dot into two parts, half Polish, half Japanese', they say. Once the mark was nailed down it was decided to use OCR-B, a monospaced font with rhomboidal roundish endings that was developed in 1968 by Adrian Frutiger for Monotype.

The red-and-white mark perfectly sums up the collaboration that brought the Warsaw-based school to life as a place of intercultural, interdisciplinary and international exchange.

POLSKO-JAPOŃSKA
AKADEMIA TECHNIK
KOMPUTEROWYCH

⊠ Zafryki: Piotr Młodożeniec
and Marek Sobczyk, 2015

Glossary

Avant garde Design that challenges the status quo.

Brand language The visual and typographical components of a specific product made under a particular name.

Branding The process of creating a complete story for a physical product or conceptual message, including its logo.

Brand name The name of a product that is represented or spelled out by a logo.

Brand narrative The story behind a branding campaign for a product or concept.

Calligraphic shape A logo comprised of sinuous or expressive handwritten brush strokes.

Comprehensive (comp) A precisely rendered visual concept (also known as a mock-up).

Corporate identity A holistic system for a business graphic personality.

Curvilinear A graphic method or style consisting of a curved line or lines (for example, art nouveau).

Development The stages in the process of creating and testing a logo or identity.

Iconic A widely recognized or famously acknowledged image, product or entity.

Integration The systematic and strategic application of a total identity.

Ligature A printed or written character consisting of two or more letters or characters joined together.

Logotype An identifying symbol, letter(s) or word(s).

Mnemonic A visual or graphic element intended to assist a person's ability to remember something.

Modular One constructed in interchangeable parts with standardized units or dimensions for flexibility and variety.

Nameplate Another word for wordmark, often the name or title of a newspaper or magazine.

Pictograph A symbol belonging to a pictorial graphic system.

Rebrand Develop a new logo and branding strategy to go with it.

Recognition The goal of a logo is to achieve recognition through positive reinforcement.

Rectilinear Letterforms or symbols characterized by straight lines.

Rollout The introduction of a logo, identity or branding system.

Refinement The process of fine-tuning or adding nuances to a logo or branding system.

Refresh To update an existing logo.

Script A style of printed letters or typefaces with graphic flourishes that resemble formal handwriting.

Shield A decorative identifying emblem (also known in heraldry as an escutcheon: wide at the top, but rounds to a point at the bottom).

Signature An identifying mark, name or symbol.

Slab serif A typeface with bold, blocky serifs.

Swash A typographical flourish, such as an exaggerated serif, terminal, tail or entry stroke.

Standards manual The official document that describes how a logo, identity or brand should be correctly employed as design components.

Strategy A blueprint or plan for how a logo, brand or identity will be used across all platforms.

Symbol A mark or character used as a substitute for representation of an object, function or process. Also a sign or word that indicates, signifies or is understood as representing an idea or relationship.

Tagline A reiterated slogan or catchphrase associated with an individual, movement, group or product.

Touchpoints A way a user can interact through a logo with a business or idea.

Trade character A graphic or illustrative embodiment in the form of animal, person or thing, sometimes comic or cartoon, that serve as mascots or fictional spokespersons developed to telegraph a particular brand narrative.

Trademark A word, name, symbol, device, or any combination of these, used to identify and distinguish the goods/services.

User experience The physical or intellectual response of an audience's relationship to a logo or brand, a product or concept.

User interface The means by which the user and an identity system interact.

Visual pun The substitution or replacement of one image for another related but surprising one, resulting in enhanced recognition.

Wordmark A trademark or logo that is made entirely from a word (usually the name of the business or company).

Further Reading

Airey, David. *Logo Design Love: A Guide to Creating Iconic Brand Identities* (2nd edition). Peachpit Press, Berkeley, Calif., 2014.

Bass, Jennifer and Kirkham, Pat. *Saul Bass: A Life in Film & Design*. Laurence King Publishing, London, 2011.

Bateman, Steven and Hyland, Angus. *Symbol*. Laurence King Publishing, London, 2014.

Bierut, Michael. *How to use graphic design to sell things, make things look better, make people laugh, make people cry, and (every once in a while) change the world*. Harper Design, New York, 2015.

Brook, Tony, Shaughnessy, Adrian and Schrauwen, Sarah; editors. *Manuals 1: Design & Identity Guidelines*. Unit Editions, London, 2014.

Cabarga, Leslie. *Logo, Font & Lettering Bible: A Comprehensive Guide to the Design, Construction and Usage of Alphabets and Symbols*. How Design Books, Cincinnati, Ohio, 2004.

Chermayeff, Ivan and Lange, Alexandra. *Identity: Chermayeff & Geismar & Haviv*. Standards Manual, New York, 2018.

Draplin, Aaron James. *Draplin Design Co: Pretty Much Everything*. Abrams, New York, 2016.

Evamy, Michael. *Logo: The Reference Guide to Symbols and Logotypes*. Laurence King Publishing, London. 2015.

Fili, Louise. *Elegantissima: The Design and Typography of Louise Fili*. Princeton Architectural Press, Hudson, New York, 2015.

Heller, Steven. *The Swastika: A Symbol Beyond Redemption?* Allworth Press, New York, 2008.

Heller, Steven and Anderson, Gail. *The graphic design idea book: Inspiration from 50 masters*. Laurence King Publishing, London, 2016.

——, *The typography idea book: Inspiration from 50 masters*. Laurence King Publishing, London, 2016.

Heller, Steven and D'Onofrio, Greg. *The Moderns: Midcentury American Graphic Design*. Abrams Books, New York, 2017.

Heller, Steven and Vienne, Véronique. *100 Ideas that Changed Graphic Design*. Laurence King Publishing, London, 2014.

Hess, Dick and Muller, Marion. *Dorfsman & CBS: A 40-year commitment to excellence in advertising and design*. America Showcase/ Rizzoli, New York, 1987.

Jacobson, Egbert (editor). *Seven Designers Look at Trademark Design*. Paul Theobald Publisher, Chicago, 1952.

Lawrence, David. *A Logo for London: The London Transport Bar and Circle*. Laurence King Publishing, London, 2013.

Millman, Debbie (editor). *Brand Bible: The Complete Guide to Building, Designing, and Sustaining Brands.* Rockport Publishers, Beverley, Massachusetts, 2012.

Mollerup, Per. *Marks of Excellence: The History and Taxonomy of Trademarks.* Phaidon Press, London, 1997.

Müller, Jens and Weideman, Julius (ed.) *Logo Modernism.* Taschen, Cologne, 2015.

Munari, Bruno. *Bruno Munari: Square, Circle, Triangle.* Princeton Architectural Press, Hudson, New York, 2016.

——, *Design as Art.* Penguin Modern Classics, New York, 2009.

Noorda, Bob. *Bob Noorda Design.* Moleskine, Milan, 2015.

Rand, Paul. *Paul Rand: A Designer's Art.* Yale University Press, New Haven, Conn., 1985.

——, *The Trademarks of Paul Rand: A Selection.* G. Wittenborn, New York, 1960.

Phaidon editors. *Graphic: 500 Designs that Matter.* Phaidon Press, London, 2017.

Rathgeb, Markus. *Otl Aicher.* Phaidon Press, London, 2015.

Snyder, Gertrude and Peckolick, Alan. *Herb Lubalin: Art Director, Graphic Designer and Typographer.* American Showcase/Rizzoli, New York, 1985.

Wozencroft, Jon. *The Graphic Language of Neville Brody.* Universe, New York, 2002.

Selected websites

Brand New:
www.underconsideration.com/brandnew

Jim Parkinson:
typedesign.com

Logoed:
www.logoed.co.uk

Logo Design Love:
www.logodesignlove.com

The Dieline:
www.thedieline.com

Index

Page numbers in **bold** refer to illustrations

Acknowledgements & picture credits

The authors are grateful to Sophie Drysdale and Deborah Hercun for their respective shepherding of this book at Laurence King Publishing. Further thanks to Christopher Westhorp for his editing and Peter Kent, our picture manager. Deep thanks to the indomitable Brian Smith for helping us locate visual and documentary materials. Without them this would have been an impossibility.

We are also appreciative to all the designers, typographers and illustrators who have allowed their work to be included.

Steven Heller and Gail Anderson

12 Copyright BRAUN P&G **15** Courtesy Catharin Noorda **16** Courtesy Studio Dumbar **19** Courtesy of International Business Machines Corporation, © International Business Machines Corporation **23** Courtesy Leica-Camera **27** © Victoria and Albert Museum **28** Stephen Doyle/Doyle Partners **31** Courtesy Lippincott **32** Courtesy think moto **35** Pearlfisher **36** Courtesy Magpie Studio **39** Images Courtesy Summa **43** SUPERO, www.supero.ch; client: Restaurant du Cercle de la Voile de Neuchâtel (Switzerland) **47** Courtesy Louise Fili **48** Original Identity System for the 2008 Campaign, Sender LLC. Sol Sender, Creative Director; Andy Keene, Designer; Amanda Gentry; Designer. Adjustments and evolution to the original mark and system, Obama Campaign Design Team: Scott Thomas, John Slabyk **51** © Volvo Trademark Holding AB. Used with permission. **52** Image courtesy Brody Associates **58** Courtesy Tarek Atrissi Design **67** © BP p.l.c. used with permission **71** LEGO logo used by courtesy of the LEGO Group **72** L'Eau d'Issey – Spring and Christmas Animations Issey Miyake 2017. Images courtesy of Philippe Apeloig/©ADAGP, Paris and DACS, London 2018 **79 top** Image courtesy Campari Archives, Davide Campari-Milano S.p.A./© DACS 2018 **78 bottom** Images courtesy Campari Archives, Davide Campari-Milano S.p.A. **80** Courtesy Roberto de Vicq **83** Courtesy Lippincott **84** Jordi Duró Studio **89** TM. & © MOURON. CASSANDRE. Lic 2018-17-09-01 www.cassandre.fr **91** Courtesy Seymour Chwast **95** Image courtesy Nathan Garland **96** Creative Directors: Malcolm Buick, Matt Owens; Strategy & Writing: Molly Carkeet; Senior Designers: Cassidy Van Dyk, Allison Connell; Designers: Sabrina Nacmias, Bora Kim; Photography: Nathan Perkel **99** © Amazon.com, Inc. **103** Courtesy Raffinerie AG **104** Courtesy Spinach Design **107** Images courtesy Heydays AS **111** Jerzy Janiszewski **112** Image courtesy Leader Creative **115** Images courtesy Lance Wyman **119** Images courtesy COLLINS, New York **121** Image courtesy Polish-Japanese Academy of Information Technology